Essential Histories

The Napoleonic Wars

The empires fight back 1808–1812

Essential Histories

The Napoleonic Wars

The empires fight back 1808–1812

Todd Fisher

OSPREY
PUBLISHING

First published in Great Britain in 2001 by Osprey Publishing,
Elms Court, Chapel Way, Botley, Oxford OX2 9LP
Email: info@ospreypublishing.com

Every attempt has been made by the Publisher to secure the
appropriate permissions for material reproduced in this book. If
there has been any oversight we will be happy to rectify the
situation and written submission should be made to the
Publishers.

ISBN 1 84176 298 9

Editor: Rebecca Cullen
Design: Ken Vail Graphic Design, Cambridge, UK
Cartography by The Map Studio
Index by Susan Williams
Picture research by Image Select International
Origination by Grasmere Digital Imaging, Leeds, UK
Printed and bound in China by L. Rex Printing Company Ltd

01 02 03 04 05   10 9 8 7 6 5 4 3 2 1

For a complete list of titles available from Osprey Publishing
please contact:

Osprey Direct UK, PO Box 140,
Wellingborough, Northants, NN8 4ZA, UK
Email: info@ospreydirect.co.uk

Osprey Direct USA,
c/o Motorbooks International, PO Box 1,
Osceola, WI 54020-0001, USA.
Email: info@ospreydirectusa.com

www.ospreypublishing.com

Contents

Introduction

The struggle for Spain

Following the Berlin Decrees of December 1806, which had established the Continental System, Napoleon sought ways to use this mainland European blockade against the British. The real hole in his net was the Iberian peninsula.

Spain, under a weak King Charles and a wicked first minister, Godoy, had been France's official ally since 1795. Spain's participation in the war had often been half-hearted, and its major contribution, its navy, had been smashed by the British at Trafalgar. Godoy had flirted with the idea of joining Prussia in 1806 and attacking France from the south. At the time, Napoleon had been embroiled in his campaign in Germany, but he had learned of the scheme and had bullied Spain into fulfilling her role as ally. He had demanded they send the cream of their army to northern Germany as Imperial support troops. Deprived of her main strike force, Spain had then had to sit out the war.

Napoleon's aim was to close off the Portuguese ports and on 21 October 1807 Godoy signed the Treaty of Fontainebleau

At the congress of Erfurt the crowned heads of Europe once again paid court to Napoleon. In this picture it is the Austrians' turn to show their submission. Talleyrand, the French foreign minister, looks on. He had already turned traitor. (Gosse, Edimedia)

allowing French troops access to Portugal via Spain. An army, under Junot, took Lisbon that November and more French troops followed into Spain.

By this time, Spain was on the verge of civil war. Two opposing camps were forming, one around the king, the other around Ferdinand, the king's son. When Ferdinand overthrew his father and arrested Godoy, both camps appealed to Napoleon for support. A conference with all parties was called in Bayonne in May 1808. Napoleon made the mistake of assuming that after the corrupt Bourbon family, the former rulers of France, the Spanish people would welcome a more liberal, efficient government. He installed his brother Joseph upon the throne.

In fact the opposite was true. Joseph was crowned in Burgos on 7 July 1808 and entered Madrid only after a Spanish revolt had been suppressed in the city. He was not to stay long. The French suffered several reverses in the field and Joseph had to evacuate Madrid soon after his arrival. By August, little of Spain was left in French hands.

Erfurt lies and spies

Napoleon planned his counter-attack. His first step was to call a meeting in Erfurt with his new ally, Tsar Alexander of Russia. Following the French victories of 1805–07, the Tsar had signed an alliance with Napoleon at Tilsit. Austria had had first chance to play this role of French ally, but had spurned the opportunity, preferring instead another attempt to regain its losses

of the last 15 years' conflict. She now stood alone on the continent among the great powers, wishing to renew the war against Napoleon.

The meeting at Erfurt, from September through October of 1808, was intended to secure the French peace while Napoleon moved into Spain to re-establish his brother Joseph on the throne. Although Alexander agreed to hold up his end of the alliance and keep an eye on Austria, he was not being sincere. Talleyrand, Napoleon's special envoy, had been plotting against Napoleon and France. Throughout the Erfurt conference he had held meetings with Alexander, urging him to feign compliance and divulging Napoleon's state secrets.

When the conference ended, Napoleon hurried south to join the army assembling along the Spanish border. France's honor was on the line, and with an eye to restoring it Napoleon began his campaign at the beginning of November. Madrid fell once again into French hands, but the effort meant that much of Napoleon's main army was now committed to the Spanish enterprise. Not only were they fighting the Spanish armies and the guerrillas, but they now had to deal with the British, who had landed an army in Portugal, under Sir Arthur Wellesley, the future Duke of Wellington.

While Napoleon was embroiled in Spain, Austria was considering her options. Still smarting from the defeats by Napoleon in 1796, 1800, and 1805, she looked for a chance of revenge. With wildly exaggerated reports of French defeats in Spain reaching the Austrians, they saw an opportunity to strike.

Chronology

1808 **6 June** Joseph Napoleon proclaimed King of Spain
27 September The start of the Congress of Erfurt
4 December Napoleon enters Madrid

1809 **9 April** The Fifth Coalition against France is proclaimed; the Austrian army attacks Bavaria
16 April Battle of Sacile
19 April Battle of Raszyn
20 April Napoleon victorious at the Battle of Abensberg
22 April Napoleon victorious at the Battle of Eckmuhl
3 May Battle of Ebelsberg
8 May Battle of the Piave
13 May Napoleon enters Vienna
21/22 May Napoleon narrowly avoids destruction at the Battle of Aspern-Essling
14 June Battle of Raab
5/6 July Napoleon victorious at the Battle of Wagram
12 July The 1809 campaign ends with the Armistice of Znaim
29 July The British land in Walcheren
17 September Peace of Frederikshamm confirms Russia's conquest of Finland from Sweden
15 December Napoleon divorces Josephine

1810 **2 April** Napoleon marries Marie-Louise, the Habsburg princess
21 August Bernadotte becomes Crown Prince of Sweden

1811 **1 December** Tsar Alexander publicly repudiates the Continental System

1812 **24 March** Secret Russo-Swedish agreement
28 May Treaty of Bucharest; Russia secures its other flank through peace with Turkey
18 June United States declares war on Britain
24 June The French army crosses the Niemen River
23 July French control of Spain shattered at the Battle of Salamanca
17–19 August The Russians evade Napoleon at the battles of Smolensk and Valutino
7 September Napoleon victorious at the Battle of Borodino
14 September The French enter Moscow; the great fire begins the next day
19 October the French army leaves Moscow
23 October the conspiracy of General Malet in Paris
24–25 October Napoleon blocked at the Battle of Maloyaroslavets
17 November Russians fail to trap the retreating French army
27–29 November Napoleon escapes the trap at the River Beresina
5 December Napoleon leaves the Grande Armée
14 December The French rearguard reaches the Niemen; end of the 1812 campaign
30 December A Prussian corps defects with the Convention of Tauroggen, the beginning of the 1813 campaign

Napoleon at the Battle of Borodino, 7 September 1812, by
Robert Alexander Hillingford. (Nassau County Museum)

Mutiny and defiance

Napoleon's popularity at home was at a low point. The treaty of Tilsit in 1807 had brought hopes of peace, but less than a year later here was France at war again, this time with Spain. A plot to overthrow Napoleon and place Murat on the throne had been hatched by Talleyrand and Fouché, Napoleon's minister of police. Napoleon had learned of this and dismissed Talleyrand. Fouché was left in place with a warning, but in later years the Emperor's leniency would come back to haunt him.

While this plot was suppressed, numerous acts of Royalist terrorism continued, primarily in Normandy and Brittany. These staunchly Catholic provinces were fertile areas of discontent. Napoleon's relationship with the Pope, Pius VII, had seriously deteriorated since the coronation of 1804. Following his annexation of the Papal lands in 1809 Napoleon was excommunicated. He retaliated by having the Pope arrested and imprisoned for five years.

To add to Napoleon's troubles at home, a romantic nationalist revival, centered in Heidelberg, had grown strong enough to cause repeated uprisings against the French throughout the German states. In the

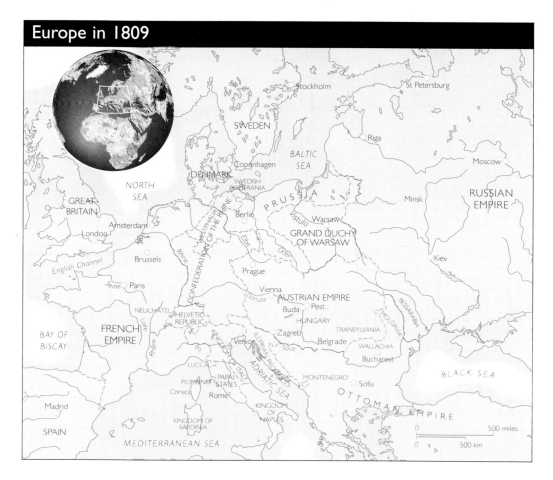

Europe in 1809

autumn of 1808 the Austrian emperor, Francis, toured his holdings accompanied by his young third wife. He received a rapturous welcome wherever he went. A war party had developed and was beating the drum to regain the Hapsburg honor by declaring war on France. So Austria put out feelers to Russia and Prussia to become allies. Russia eventually agreed to take no action against Austria, despite pretending to remain Napoleon's ally, and Prussia originally agreed to provide 80,000 men to aid in the effort.

Austria seeks reprisal

The commander of the Hapsburg forces was the Archduke Charles, Emperor Francis' brother. He had been the leader of the peace party and still had strong reservations about taking on Napoleon. Charles had been trying to reform the army ever since the defeat of Austerlitz in 1805. Much had been accomplished, but his efforts had been severely frustrated by court politics and he felt that much more was needed before they were ready to challenge the French. However, the war party was too strong, and Charles faced the choice of agreeing to the war or resigning. He chose the former.

If Austria had counted on Russian support, she was to be disappointed. Russia was successfully waging two different wars at the beginning of 1809 – with Turkey and with Sweden. Furthermore, she was ostensibly at war with Britain, though neither side was actually willing to fight. Britain had sent a large portion of its army to Gothenburg to support the Swedes, but this was not where the fighting was taking place, since all the battles were in Finland. While the Swedes fought bravely, the might of Russia brought them to the negotiating table and the Swedes were forced to trade Finland for peace.

Prussia was still led by the weak-willed King Frederick Wilhelm. Although initially he promised help to Austria, he lost his nerve and backed out before the shooting started.

Only Britain would lend support to the Hapsburg army. At first she hesitated, but once it became clear that the Austrians were in earnest, money was promised and a vague assurance given of a landing on the north coast of Europe. This was all the determined men around Francis needed to prepare for war. A report from the finance minister to Francis stated that the treasury would run out of money by mid 1809 if the army remained mobilized. It was reasoned therefore that while the army was there, it should be used. The thought that Austria should demobilize seems never to have occurred to the Austrian high command. Even Charles, while warning that the army was not yet prepared for war, did not wish to have his reformed troops demobilized.

The Austrian foreign minister to France was Prince Metternich. He made every effort to appear cordial to the French but spied and plotted with the likes of Talleyrand to undermine Napoleon. Metternich had an abiding hatred of everything for which Napoleon stood. An aristocrat of the old school, he saw Napoleon as the embodiment of the Revolution and a direct threat to his way of life. He spied successfully on the French court and gave accurate reports to Vienna of Napoleon's preparations and reactions to the Austrian mobilization. In large part, however, his warnings went unheeded.

Napoleon, meanwhile, behaved as if in a swirling mist, appearing to see clearly one moment and be completely in the dark the next. He had faith in his Russian ally, and was sure that the threat of a two-front war on Austria would deter any hostilities. However, he began to mobilize another army to meet the threat from the east. He withdrew men from Spain and called on the Confederation of the Rhine states to bring their contingents up to full war footing. He called up the recruit class of 1810 to fill his ranks. In all the theaters facing Austria he would field over 400,000 men. The Austrians had estimated his strength at only half that number.

France, Austria, and Russia

The French army

Napoleon had invaded Spain with most of his veterans from the glorious campaigns of 1805–07. When Austria threatened in 1809, he could only afford to recall his Guard and a few extra troops to meet the threat. These joined with Davout's and Marmont's veteran corps. The remainder of the army was made up of newly formed troops and various allies.

With all the demands being made upon the Empire, Napoleon had to rely increasingly upon his client states to provide manpower. Northern Italy, Bavaria, Saxony, Westphalia, Wurttemberg, Holland, and the Grand Duchy of Warsaw (Poland) each provided a corps, while other lesser states sent smaller contingents. Many of these troops saw serious fighting throughout the campaign. The remainder of the army was created by calling up the conscription classes early. On the whole the army was a grade down from previous campaigns.

The structure of the army had not fundamentally changed. The corps system was in place and all corps were led by quality fighting generals. Napoleon's infantry regiments were divided into two main classes: line (*ligne*) and light (*légère*). These were essentially identical in function, with the light perhaps getting more skirmishing duties. A regiment had two or three field battalions, with a fourth depot battalion called up to complete the new formations. Battalions were transformed from nine companies to six, leaving four center companies, one light, and one grenadier company per battalion. This demanded less training in field maneuvers.

Unlike the infantry, Napoleon's cavalry was at its height in 1809. After incorporating the superior horses captured during 1806–07, the units were expanded and improved,

most notably the 30 regiments of dragoons which were transformed from mediocre to formidable. The cuirassiers had expanded too and had received additional training to make them a powerful breakthrough force. They held the advantage over their Austrian counterparts in number and in armor, having both front and back plates while the Austrians had only front.

The French light cavalry, hussars and chasseurs, gained a reputation for battlefield prowess, but their scouting skills were poor and Napoleon was often left blind as to the whereabouts of the enemy.

The artillery had been reformed since 1804. The Gribeauval system was replaced by the *An XI* (Year 11) models. These put 12lb and 6lb guns in place of the 12lb, 8lb, and 4lb guns of the former system (the weight referring to the cannonball used). The new carriages were lighter and more mobile, standardized to include the field guns and howitzers. This made for more efficient artillery parks. Although not all of the older guns had been replaced, the process was well under way. As the campaign progressed, a number of captured Austrian guns were added to the reserves. The artillery had been Napoleon's arm as a young lieutenant, and as a result many talented men sought out this branch of service. This resulted in the French artillery being unquestionably the best in Europe.

The Guard Corps was made up of all three arms. The infantry had the new regiments of the Young and Middle Guard added to their number. These new formations, while not having the prestige of the Old Guard, served very well during the campaign.

The Guard Cavalry gained the Polish Light Horse. These Poles had added a lance to their equipment following Wagram, where they had fought a regiment of Austrian lancers (*Uhlans*) and taken several lances as trophies. The other regiments of the Chasseurs and Grenadiers à Cheval and Empress Dragoons, and the sub-units of Mameluks and Gendarmes, made up the most feared cavalry in the world. Although rarely used, their effect was devastating.

There were two types of artillery of the Guard: horse artillery (*Volante*) and heavy foot, nicknamed Napoleon's 'beautiful daughters'. The horse could fly into position and produce an incredible amount of firepower at a critical point; the heavy guns could outshoot any enemy artillery and pulverize opposing formations.

The Confederation of the Rhine troops were organized upon either the French or German model but gradually all adopted the French six-company formations. The troops were of variable quality but usually adequate. The cavalry was usually mediocre, with the exception of the Saxons, who were very good. The artillery was never up to French standards but usually well matched to the enemy.

Napoleon's army in 1809 was good, but nowhere near the quality of the French army at Austerlitz in 1805. As Napoleon prepared for the invasion of Russia he pulled troops from every available source. In addition to the Confederation, Italians, and Polish troops used in 1809, he incorporated the Kingdom of Naples and Spanish troops. Furthermore, his reluctant allies, Prussia and Austria, sent a corps each to the front.

There is little to distinguish Napoleon's armies of 1809 and 1812 other than increased size of the latter. Regiments acquired a 4th, 5th, or even 6th field battalion, cavalry regiments were brought up to an average of six squadrons, and a new class of light cavalry was introduced – lancers. These were converted dragoon regiments. There was no change in the artillery batteries except that they were given their full complement of men. In all, the army that started out in 1812 was the largest Napoleon had ever assembled and showed the variations in quality expected in such an all-out muster of force.

The Austrian army

Austerlitz and the subsequent Treaty of Pressburg were further confirmation that the Austrian army needed an overhaul. The obvious choice for the job was Emperor Francis' brother, Archduke Charles, who was acknowledged to be the finest general in the realm. However, Francis mistrusted his brother because Napoleon had offered Charles the Austrian throne following Austerlitz. While Charles had loyally refused, the seeds of fear had been planted and Francis kept the Military Advisory Board (*Hofkriegsrat*) in place to oversee his brother's activities as supreme commander. This led to an atmosphere of mistrust and a situation in which the two camps spied on each other, initiating a series of court intrigues. This further slowed a reform process which was already hampered by a natural Habsburg conservatism.

Between 1806 and 1808 the Habsburg empire swung back and forth between calls to join a war effort against France and the peace party, led by Charles, who said more time was needed to complete the army reforms. By the end of 1808 the war party gained the upper hand when the Habsburgs interpreted Napoleon's Spanish woes as a chance for revenge. Thus the country began preparations for war.

In 1806 Charles had issued a new guide to army and unit tactics. Changes were small and incremental, yet in the context of the entrenched attitudes in Austria they were seen as very advanced. The primary tactical reform was the 'mass'. This was an anti-cavalry infantry formation created by closing up the spacing between ranks. This modest tactical device was rarely used outside of the immediate sight of Archduke Charles, reflecting the reluctance of the generals to try anything new.

Following the defeats of Ulm and Austerlitz, Mack's earlier 'reforms' were considered to have been a failure in action and Charles abandoned the four-company battalion and returned to the six-company formation used prior to the 1805 campaign.

The army was divided into five categories of infantry: Line, Grenzer, Grenadier, Jaeger, and Landwehr.

The Line had 61 regiments (46 German and 15 Hungarian). Each was made up of three battalions.

The Grenzers from Croatia had 17 regiments with two field battalions and one reserve battalion. The skirmish skills of the mountain troops had slowly eroded and by 1809 there was little difference between mountain troops and Line regiments.

Hungarian and Austrian infantry. (Ottenfeld)

The Grenadier battalions were officially composed of companies taken from the Line regiments, but by 1809 they had in effect become separate formations. These were the elite of the army and were brigaded into their own shock formations.

The Jaegers – elite rifle-armed troops – had taken on the army's skirmishing duties and performed very well throughout the campaign. With only nine battalions, they left the Austrians woefully short of skirmishers to match their French opponents.

The Landwehr was sub-divided into volunteer and militia units. This measure had been considered for many years, but had always been shelved for fear of arming the general populace. By 1809, however, it was clear that new sources of manpower would have to be found to fight the war and even this new plan would only provide a portion of what was needed; only the volunteer units showed much value in combat.

Charles' cavalry remained largely unchanged. Efforts to expand the number or capacity of the mounted arm were curtailed for economic reasons. In general, this left the Austrians' *arme blanche* outnumbered and outclassed. The cavalry's efforts were further undermined by the practice of distributing it in small units throughout the army. This left only the Cuirassiers as a massed force for shock purposes. These eight regiments of breast-plated cavalry would prove too little to make a decisive impact in battle.

The Austrian artillery, once the finest in the world, had fallen behind the times. Charles sought to reform this arm and re-organized the cannon into more effective batteries. He militarized the transport service – a marked improvement – but still the doctrine of massing guns at the point of decision was one which was followed more in theory than practice; although Aspern-Essling would be the best day for the Austrian artillery in the entire war, such massed artillery tactics were not institutionalized. The weight of the Austrian shot was less than that of their French counterparts and

Hungarian Grenadiers. (Ottenfeld)

therefore lacked hitting power. Finally, there was no prestige to the artillery so the best officers gravitated to other arms.

Charles imitated the superior French model of the corps structure, but not in time to familiarize the commanders with its workings and possibilities. Used to a rigid structure, often based on elaborate planning and long-winded written orders, the Austrian corps commanders remained fixed in place, waiting for orders rather than taking advantage of the resources at their disposal.

The General Staff was in a constant state of reform, yet change came at a snail's pace. The average field general was in his sixties – a marked contrast to the youthful French. The older the general, the less likely they were to lead from the front. This gave them a greater chance of survival, but lessened their ability to react. An additional problem was the small number of staff at army and corps level, which meant that changes to orders were not always possible in the time available.

The Russian army

The Russians had been fierce but lumbering opponents of Napoleon in 1805–07. They had defended well, but had been unable to match the French in a battle of maneuver. Following the Peace of Tilsit it was clear that the organization inherited from the Seven Years' War needed to be overhauled.

This task was originally given to Alexei Arakcheev, a sadistic martinet who showed little interest in reform except in his artillery. He replaced the old, slow-moving artillery with lighter, better, 12- and 6-pounders and improved the Licorne, the Russian answer to the howitzer. These new models still lacked the mobility and hitting power of the French, but they were a marked improvement.

Arakcheev did little else to change the army other then terrorize his contemporaries and give his favorites positions of power. In almost all matters he was a reactionary and a xenophobe, so he did the Tsar a great service when he resigned in 1810 over a power struggle. His replacement was Barclay de Tolly, who reorganized the army and introduced a corps structure similar to that of the French. He also tried to install a staff system like Napoleon's but with less success.

The army of near a million men was scattered over the vast Russian empire. Many were in depots and many more were levies waiting to be called up. In the field at the start of 1812, there were over 600,000 men, equal to Napoleon's entire force, with another 500,000 men waiting to be called up. However, mobilizing this army would prove to be a lengthy process, so initially Russia faced Napoleon with only a third of his force.

The Russian infantry was obedient and stalwart. The officers lacked imagination and initiative, but the peasant infantrymen, used to hardship, had few complaints about a military lifestyle that was often draconian and they fought hard when put into battle. The infantry was particularly adept at digging in when in defense, offering tenacious resistance, and enduring a heavy pounding from the superior French artillery.

The infantry was divided into three types: line, jaegers, and grenadiers. The line and jaegers were essentially the same, designated for light infantry duties but ill-trained for the job (although at Borodino almost all the Jaeger regiments broke down into skirmish formation). The grenadiers were sub-divided into two types: grenadier regiments and converged grenadier battalions. The regiments were true elite formations that had earned their title on the battlefield and continued to justify this honor. The converged battalions were a merger of companies taken from the line regiments and elevated to elite status. These men were good, reliable troops, but not markedly better than their brethren in the line.

The cavalry, the most aristocratic of the Russian arms, had needed least by way of reform. It was organized into permanent divisions and had begun to practice large formation maneuvers when the war broke out. The cavalry was steady if unremarkable. It performed well against many of the allied

Charge! Hurrah! Hurrah! by V. Vereshchagin. An idealized picture of Russian Grenadiers going into the attack.

the battlefield and amassed as much as possible for the battle of Eylau in 1807, providing a frightful example of the carnage Russian cannon could inflict. While Russian officers had not developed Napoleon's skill in deploying huge batteries on the move, they firmly believed in pounding an opponent into submission.

Finally there was the Russian Guard. This combined arms formation, modeled upon Napoleon's Guard, was made up of elite formations. They received the best of everything Russia could provide and were the Tsar's shock troops. None in the world could match them, save the French. They were used more liberally than Napoleon's Guard, because to do so never risked the entire regime.

It was in command that the Russians failed most. Rivalry and bickering led to a series of near-disastrous appointments. Often generals were put in place more for their political acumen than their military skills and were replaced because of a loss of political influence rather than for any failure. The responsibility for this lay with the Tsar, but even he was often looking over his shoulder, fearful of a coup!

troops, but usually gave way when matched against an equal number of French. In these encounters, their lack of training above the squadron level proved costly.

The one cavalry force that made a real difference on campaign was the Cossacks. These steppe horsemen could outmarch any of their rivals and they were mounted on sturdy ponies which could withstand the hardships of the Russian weather and terrain. While rarely useful against anything approaching an equal number of cavalry, they were a nightmare to stragglers and scouts, and could occasionally destroy smaller isolated enemy units. The lure of booty made them lose discipline, but they were ready to attack to find their loot if the odds were good. In 1812 Cossacks appeared in great numbers.

The artillery was the backbone of the army. The Russians were the first to recognize the changing role of artillery on

The Austrian campaign to the march on Moscow

The Austrians invade Bavaria

With the decision to go to war made, Archduke Charles planned the main Austrian advance along the upper Danube River. The 1st through 5th Corps, along with the 1st Reserve Corps, would advance north of the river out of Bohemia. The 6th Corps and the 2nd Reserve Corps would advance south of the river from a starting position on the Bavarian border. When reports arrived that the French were beginning to concentrate in the Augsburg area, the specter of an unprotected Vienna being taken by a rapid advance along the south bank of the Danube caused Charles to rethink his plans. Accordingly, he shifted the main body of his troops south of the Danube to the Inn River line on the border with Bavaria. While this countered the perceived threat, the decision cost the Austrians one month of critical time. Even so, by 10 April 1809, the army was in position.

On other fronts, Archduke Ferdinand was to lead the 8th Corps and additional troops against Napoleon's Polish allies in the Galicia region, while Archduke John with the 8th and 9th Corps would attack the French and Northern Italian army commanded by Napoleon's stepson, Prince Eugene de Beauharnais. The Austrians believed that by applying broad and constant pressure, French resources would be stretched to breaking point.

Napoleon believed that he had until mid-April to concentrate his forces, but left Marshal Berthier instructions to fall back on the lines of communications should an attack come earlier. Berthier, a superlative chief of staff, struggled when commanding an army. When crucial orders from Napoleon were delayed, Berthier's confusion only worsened.

Archduke Charles was considered the only general who could match Napoleon, but he was prone to inaction at the most inappropriate times. (Roger-Viollet)

In the early morning of 10 April, the leading elements of the Austrian army crossed the Inn River. The opposing cordon of Bavarians fell back, but bad roads and freezing rain delayed the Austrian offensive during the first week. The Bavarians made a brief stand on the Isar River at Landshut on 16 April, before once more retreating and yielding the passage of the critical river line. Beyond the Bavarians, only Marshal Davout's 3rd Corps, deployed around Regensburg, remained guarding the key bridge over the Danube that linked the north and south banks.

Charles stopped to analyze the intelligence he had received on the evening

of 17 April. By concentrating his forces north
of the Danube and delivering a thrust from
the south, Charles could drive Davout's
forces back and the whole of the French
defensive position would come unhinged.
The archduke ordered the two wings of the
Wurttemberg army to converge on
Regensburg, but his plans had to be altered
the following day when he learned that
Davout was heading south along the Danube
and attempting to link up with supporting
French corps further to the south and west.
Davout had been placed in this precarious
position through a combination of bad luck
and poor timing, and Charles had a golden
opportunity to crush the 'Iron Marshal' by
pinning his 3rd Corps against the river.

The arrival of Napoleon

Napoleon arrived at Donauworth, the French
headquarters, on 17 April 1809. He
immediately began to assess the disastrous
situation facing his army. Until now the
French army had been badly out-scouted by
the numerically superior Austrian cavalry.
The most reliable reports were coming from
spies and civilians reporting to Davout's
men. The 3rd Corps was clearly in extreme
danger, and aid could not arrive for a couple
of days. The best solution seemed to be for
Davout to abandon his position around
Regensburg and link up with the Bavarians
further to the east. Unfortunately, when
these orders from Napoleon arrived, Davout
required an additional day to gather up his
corps as they were scattered and fatigued
from marching and counter-marching as a
result of Berthier's confused orders. Davout
set off early on the morning of 19 April to
link up with his allies.

Davout's 3rd Corps moved south out of
Regensburg on the direct road that ran along
the Danube and toward Ingolstadt. In the
initial stages of this maneuver his corps,
formed in two parallel columns of march,
were strung out with no line of retreat if the
Austrians attacked from the east. Davout had
left a regiment behind the walls of

Regensburg to prevent any passage of the
Danube by the Austrians and to protect his
rear. Charles' plan of attack was to wheel
with his 3rd Corps attacking along the
Danube while the 4th and 1st Reserve Corps
swung on the pivot.

Teugen-Hausen

On the morning of 19 April, both armies got
under way, the French with a two-hour head
start. By 8.30 am, Davout had nearly escaped
the trap. Two of his four divisions had
moved past the choke point, but the marshal
received word of strong enemy activity
moving up from the south and his supply
train was not yet through the key village of
Teugen. The Austrian 3rd Corps, under Field-
Marshal the Prince of Hohenzollern, was
rapidly arriving upon the battlefield and
trying to cut them off. This force had been
partially weakened out of fear that the
Bavarians might fall upon their flank so
more than one division had been detached
to act as a flank guard. These men would be
sorely missed in the day's contest.

The action opened with the French
skirmishers being thrown back toward
Teugen as the advance guard of the Austrian
3rd Corps crashed forward. Davout, realizing
that his flanks were in peril, sent the
103rd Line forward to buy time and give the
remainder of St Hilaire's division a chance
to deploy. He sent them in skirmish order
toward the town of Hausen and the
6,000 Austrians waiting for them. At the
same time, Davout ordered Friant's division
to advance to St Hilaire's left and support
the effort. Friant had his own problems:
elements of the Austrian 4th Corps were
going in to the attack as well. However,
fortunately for the French, at the rear of the
column, General Montbrun's cavalry would
mesmerize Field-Marshal Rosenberg's
4th Corps for most of the day.

The men of the 103rd were doing well
considering they were outnumbered three to
one and all the artillery on the field was
Habsburg. As they finally gave way, the

'Terrible 57th', arguably the finest regiment of line infantry in the French army, swung into action. They took a position upon the ridge overlooking the town and the Austrian assault ground to a halt.

Now checked, the Austrians failed to see the 10th Light Regiment creep up through the woods. This elite force fell upon the Austrian artillery and drove it from the field. Hohenzollern committed some of his reserves in response to this reverse, and as the white-coated Austrians came forward, they tipped the balance back to their side in this running fight. Davout had to commit all available troops on the field to stem the tide.

Sensing victory, more Austrians were released and this time cavalry charged the beleaguered 57th, which lay down a withering fire and formed square with its flank battalion. The battered cavalry withdrew and played no further part in the day's actions. Under the cover of this cavalry assault, a fresh regiment came up to attack the French line. The Manfredini regiment advanced in column through a swale in the ground and turned on the flank of the

One of Napoleon's aides, Mouton, stormed the bridge at Landshut despite the defended barricade and buildings. Napoleon was so impressed he punned, 'My Mouton (sheep in French) is a lion.' (Roger-Viollet)

57th. Fortunately for Davout, General Compans saw what was about to happen and led newly arriving troops forward. The two columns collided and the French came off better. The Austrians fell back, rallied, and came on again, led by the dashing General Alois Liechtenstein. The 57th, out of ammunition, finally gave way. The French fell off the ridge and down to the town of Teugen. There Davout rallied the men and, sending in his last reserve, retook the ridgeline. The Austrians were almost completely played out on the ridge, when Friant's men appeared upon their right flank. This was too much, and the Habsburg line gave way. Streaming down the ridgeline toward the town of Hausen, they rallied behind the last reserves that Hohenzollern had to commit on the field.

Once more General Liechtenstein led the attack, carrying the Wurzburg regiment's

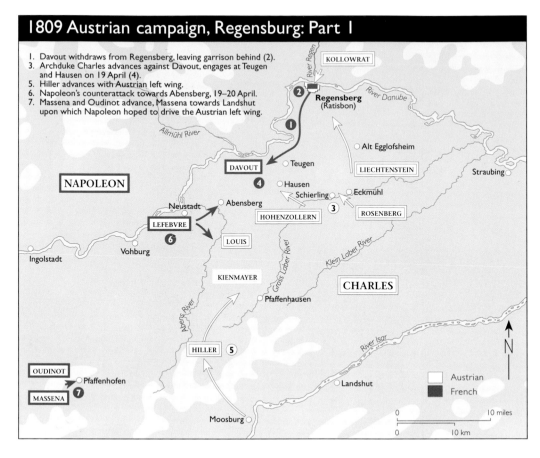

1809 Austrian campaign, Regensburg: Part 1

1. Davout withdraws from Regensberg, leaving garrison behind (2).
3. Archduke Charles advances against Davout, engages at Teugen and Hausen on 19 April (4).
5. Hiller advances with Austrian left wing.
6. Napoleon's counterattack towards Abensberg, 19–20 April.
7. Massena and Oudinot advance, Massena towards Landshut upon which Napoleon hoped to drive the Austrian left wing.

(IR 3) flag to inspire the men, and stormed the woods. While his attack drove back the French line, more of Friant's men and the arrival of the long-awaited French artillery restored the situation. For his efforts, General Liechtenstein lay severely wounded. The Austrians had retreated behind the protection of their guns deployed in front of Hausen when a violent thunderstorm started and the battle ended.

Davout had defeated a force twice his size and had been able to re-open communications with the rest of Napoleon's army. Charles had spent the battle only a couple of miles away with a reserve of 12 elite grenadier battalions. It is difficult to determine who was at fault for the failure to commit these troops. Clearly, communication was poor, but the blame must be shared between Hohenzollern for not begging for the men and Charles for not finding out what was happening to his front. As it was, the Austrians knew they had fought well but had still lost: demoralization began to set in.

As the battle of Teugen-Hausen was drawing to a close, Napoleon switched to the attack. He ordered Marshal Masséna's 4th Corps to advance on Landshut. Masséna advanced from Ingolstadt with the heavy cavalry, linked up with the Bavarians and Wurttembergers, and ordered the 2nd Corps to hurry to the front. By 9.00 am the following day he was in place. To give him even more flexibility Napoleon made an ad hoc corps from two of Davout's divisions and placed it under Marshal Jean Lannes, who had just arrived from Spain. Davout and his two remaining divisions would press the forces in front of him.

Napoleon's plan was to drive the Austrians back to Landshut, which he assumed was their line of communication. There they would be pinned by Masséna's Corps coming up from the south.

The battle of Abensberg, 20 April 1809, was a running battle, with the Austrians

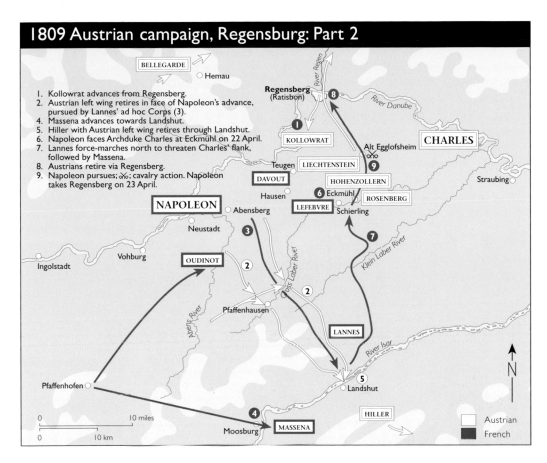

1809 Austrian campaign, Regensburg: Part 2

1. Kollowrat advances from Regensberg.
2. Austrian left wing retires in face of Napoleon's advance, pursued by Lannes' ad hoc Corps (3).
3. Massena advances towards Landshut.
4. Hiller with Austrian left wing retires through Landshut.
5. Napoleon faces Archduke Charles at Eckmühl on 22 April.
6. Lannes force-marches north to threaten Charles' flank, followed by Massena.
7. Austrians retire via Regensberg.
8. Napoleon pursues; ✕; cavalry action. Napoleon takes Regensberg on 23 April.

(Map labels: BELLEGARDE, Hemau, Regensberg (Ratisbon), River Regen, River Danube, KOLLOWRAT, CHARLES, Alt Egglofsheim, LIECHTENSTEIN, Teugen, HOHENZOLLERN, Straubing, DAVOUT, Eckmühl, ROSENBERG, Hausen, LEFEBVRE, Schierling, NAPOLEON, Abensberg, Neustadt, Klein Laber River, Vohburg, OUDINOT, Gross Laber River, Ingolstadt, Pfaffenhausen, LANNES, Abens River, River Isar, Pfaffenhofen, Landshut, HILLER, N, Austrian, French, Moosburg, MASSENA, 0 10 miles, 0 10 km)

being driven back throughout the day. By nightfall the Austrian 5th, 6th, and 2nd Reserve Corps were well on their way to Landshut. They arrived the following morning, having marched through most of the night. General Hiller, commander of the Austrians in this sector, did his best to put them in good defensive positions.

Napoleon was close on their heels. At Landshut, on 21 April, Napoleon assembled his forces and attacked through the town and over the two bridges that spanned the Isar River. This daring assault saw more than 8,000 Austrians surrounded and forced to surrender in the town. Strategically the attack may have been irrelevant, because the Austrian position had already been flanked by the French 4th Corps. Masséna's men crossed over the river quickly, closing on the position from the south. They narrowly missed cutting off the retreating Austrians who had been foiled by bad roads, a lack of initiative in the

Davout (Job). At Auerstadt in 1806 and at Eckmühl in 1809 Davout proved to be tough enough to score victories over superior numbers of enemies. (Edimedia)

aging marshal, and pockets of determined enemy resistance. Compromised by the hard-driving French offensive, this Austrian wing fell back to the east and to the next defensive line.

Early next morning, Napoleon received the last of several desperate messages from Davout. This time the news was delivered by the trusted General Piré, who finally managed to persuade the Emperor that he did not face the main Habsburg army. Napoleon now grasped that his left flank stood in the greatest peril.

Throughout 21 April, Davout attacked the retreating Austrians with the help of a Bavarian division under Marshal Lefebvre. The further back the Austrians fell, the stronger their line became, for in fact they were falling back on their main force. General Montbrun's cavalry, off to the north, was reporting massive formations heading Davout's way. The combat on the first day of the Battle of Eckmühl, as this fight was to become known, was sharp, with each side giving as much as they took. However, that night Davout faced a terrible predicament. While a fresh division had come up to his support and the artillery train would be present for any fighting in the morning, his infantry was low on ammunition. Davout

knew that at least three Austrian corps remained in front of him. In fact the situation was even more desperate than he realized, for Regensburg had fallen and two more Austrian corps would be able to cross the Danube and enter the fight.

Charles saw this great opportunity, but his spread-out army would take half a day to get into position. He, like his opponent, was reading the situation wrongly. He assumed that Davout was the leading element of the main French army. Charles' forces were aligned on a north-south axis, and his reinforcements were coming from the north, through Regensburg. If the plan worked, his new arrivals would fall upon the French far left flank. The archduke wanted the two wings of his army to coordinate with each other, so he would allow the French to expend themselves upon his defensive position around Eckmühl and take no offensive action himself until his reinforcements were in position.

Eckmühl

As dawn broke on 22 April, the two sides faced each other and except for some skirmishing, neither side made an attack. Morning turned to midday and still an uneasy calm hung over the battlefield.

While Charles looked for signs of his 2nd Corps, Davout had a better grasp of the developing situation. Napoleon had sent General Piré back with the message that the Emperor was coming with his army. Davout was to maintain contact and expect Napoleon to launch his attack at 3.00 pm. Every minute that Charles delayed increased the marshal's chances of survival and victory.

At about 1.00 pm the leading elements of the Austrian attack collided with Montbrun's cavalry. The hilly and wooded terrain great aided the French in slowing down the impetus of the attack. As the French horsemen retreated, the Austrian commander of the left flank, General Rosenberg, felt concern as he observed Davout's main force opposite him. Instead of quickly shifting to meet the threat caused by Charles' attack, they remained in place and were watching him! Rosenberg knew this could mean only one thing. He began to shift troops to meet a threat from the south. It was not long before his suspicions were confirmed. His small flank guard had caved in under a massive French force that was heading his way.

Napoleon had achieved a most remarkable march, one of the finest examples of turning on an army's axis in all of history. After receiving the intelligence at

The outnumbered Austrian cavalry attempted to delay the pursuing French.

around 2.00 am he had set into motion the orders to turn his army to the north and to march the 18 miles to the help of his beleaguered marshal. In short order, the plans were set in motion. Remarkably, Napoleon would arrive even earlier than promised.

The tip of his hammer blow was General Vandamme and his Wurttemberg troops. These Germans came on with the greatest élan. Led by their crack light battalion, they stormed across the bridge at Eckmühl and into the town. There they seized the chateau despite dogged Austrian resistance.

As the first of Napoleon's attacks got under way, Davout launched his own attack against the center of Rosenberg's position, the village of Unterlaiching and the woods above. Davout had sent in the 10th Legere to carry out the task. This elite unit paused only momentarily in the village before continuing on against the woods. There they faced several times their own number, and a vicious fight ensued tree to tree. Eventually, Davout reinforced the efforts of the light infantry regiment with the Bavarians under General Deroy and the position was taken.

To the north of Unterlaiching, Davout's men under Friant and the remaining troops of St Hilaire slowly pushed back the defenders around Oberlaiching and the woods to its north. A redoubt held by Hungarian grenadiers was overrun, the whole line began to give way, and Charles ordered a retreat.

Between the town of Eckmühl and the woods above Unterlaiching was a ridgeline called the Bettelberg. Astride the ridge was some of the best cavalry in the Austrian Empire, including the Vincent Chevaulegers and the Stipsic Hussars, and several batteries of guns. After deploying on the marshy plain below, the Bavarian and Wurttemberg light cavalry launched a charge uphill against the position. Briefly overrunning one of the batteries, they were thrown back by the two crack cavalry regiments of Hussars and Chevaulegers. The countercharging Austrians were in turn stopped by the Bavarian infantry.

A stand-off developed. The Austrians were determined to hold this position until the rest of the army got away, and Napoleon was equally determined to break the position and destroy the retreating adversary. To accomplish this goal, Napoleon now committed his heavy cavalry. The divisions of St Sulpice and Nansouty deployed in the soft ground. Their ranks were pummeled as they maneuvered under the continuously firing heavy guns on the Bettelberg. Slowly the magnificent cavalry moved forward, picking up speed. As they hit the ridge and began to ascend the heights, they were in a full canter. Finally, in the last hundred paces they broke into a gallop. The tired, outnumbered Austrian cavalry was overthrown and the heavy guns were taken. The lighter guns limbered and broke away, and many of their gunners were sabered. Now established on the ridge, the cuirassiers stopped to catch their breath. Others would have to do the immediate follow-up.

The French victory had been won by late afternoon, but Charles was able to pull off his infantry with few captured. While the French organized their pursuit, the Austrians found a choke point in the road to buy time. Napoleon urged on his troops and sent his heavy cavalry into the van to run down the enemy. They caught up with Charles' final rearguard a couple of miles from Regensburg at Alt Egglofsheim.

What followed was an enormous cavalry clash. Charles had left cuirassiers and his now exhausted light cavalry to delay the French. Napoleon committed his three divisions of cuirassiers with the support of Bavarian and Wurttemberg light cavalry. The French swept down, but the Austrian heavies were fresh and plowed into the French with great effect. The entire fight turned into a swirling melee, with each side feeding in more and more troopers. The Austrians fought magnificently and for a while more than held their own with the exhausted French, but in the end the French superiority in numbers was too much. Seeing more French appear and realizing that it was quickly becoming dark, the Austrians tried to break off. It was at this moment that the next wave of oncoming French shattered the tired Austrians. Panic resulted and the frantic horsemen streamed back toward Regensburg and the safety of her walls. The French too became confused in the gloom and the pursuit was ineffectual. This was lucky for the Archduke Charles, since he had been swept up in the rout.

Napoleon is wounded

The following day, 23 April, found the Austrians retreating as fast as possible over the Danube and the protection of her left bank. A sizable rearguard was left to defend the walls of Regensburg. Napoleon was disappointed when he learned that the French garrison had fallen. He had hoped to trap the Austrians against the river. Instead he launched a massive assault in an attempt to catch as much of the retreating army as possible. The medieval walls would easily fall to a prolonged bombardment, but time was short. Napoleon's infantry rushed forward with ladders to scale the walls. Each time the firepower of the Austrians drove them back. At the height of the battle, a bullet struck Napoleon in the heel. Rumors spread quickly amongst the French that he had been seriously hurt. Wishing to stop the panic, he had his wound quickly bandaged and rode along the lines to show himself. A crisis was averted.

Even with the panic quelled, every renewed assault was driven back. Finally, the fiery Marshal Lannes grabbed a ladder and exclaimed: 'I was a grenadier before I was a marshal, and still am!' His men, shamed into another attempt, grabbed ladders and made one final attempt. This time it succeeded and the French were in. The Austrians fought

Napoleon rode amongst his troops before Regensburg to show he was not wounded. In the background, the French are preparing to assault the city walls. (Myrbach, Roger-Viollet)

desperately in an attempt to prevent the French from working their way through the city and reaching the critical stone bridge over the Danube before Charles' engineers could destroy it. House-to-house, hand-to-hand fighting followed. Five Austrian battalions were to perish or surrender, but their sacrifice was not in vain. The French broke through to the river just in time to see the charges explode. Charles and his main army had escaped, and Napoleon had lost his opportunity for a quick knock-out blow. The following day the Emperor turned his attention to trapping and destroying the enemy forces still south of the Danube.

While developments in Bavaria saw the repulse of the main Austrian offensive, things had gone better for the House of Habsburg on other fronts. In the Tyrol region, which had been ceded to Bavaria following the disastrous Austerlitz-Ulm campaign, General Chasteler had invaded with 10,000 men and the region had risen in revolt to support his efforts. His movement was coordinated with Archduke John's invasion of Italy and Dalmatia. Chasteler had advanced on Innsbruck and captured virtually all opposing forces with the help of bands of patriotic Tyrolian rebels, whose most notable leader was Andreas Hofer. Within three days almost all of the Tyrol was retaken by the Austrians. It would be May before any response could be organized.

Actions in Italy

Archduke John's army advanced against Napoleon's stepson, the viceroy of Italy, Prince Eugene de Beauharnais. Although the Franco-Italian army outnumbered John's, it was scattered throughout northern Italy. This was Napoleon's fault, for he had believed that the Austrians would not attack until later, if at all, and that to assemble the army ahead of time would in itself have been a provocation which might have ignited a war. This meant that as John advanced, only about half of Eugene's troops were available at the battlefield of Sacile on 15/16 April

1809. Eugene was aching for a fight, in order to 'win his spurs.' Furthermore, Chasteler's success was threatening his northern flank, and he felt that if he could defeat John, he could deal with the threat in the Tyrol at his leisure.

The first day of the battle saw John maul Eugene's advance guard at Pordenone. The following day, Eugene tried an outflanking attack that became bogged down in the soggy, broken terrain. John calmly watched as the French spent themselves trying to seize the village of Porcia. Once it had finally been taken, after several attempts, the Austrians launched an attack against the French left and drove it back against the Livenza River. Staring at the threat to his line of retreat, Eugene broke off the battle. Marching through the rain-soaked night, Eugene's army outpaced the lackluster Austrians in pursuit.

After several stands to make a rearguard, Eugene fell back to Verona and the line of the Adige River. On this familiar ground, held by the French in 1796 under Napoleon and 1805 under Masséna, Eugene gathered his army together and prepared to go over to the offensive.

Other fronts

In Dalmatia, Marmont, under the nominal command of Eugene, was told to attack the enemy in front of him. His mountain offensive on 30 April was repulsed by General Stoichewich's force, with most of the serious damage being caused by the skilled mountain troops, the Grenzer. The French retreat that followed was harassed by locals who sprang several ambushes.

To the north, things were going equally badly for Napoleon's allies. Prince Poniatowski had tried to stop Archduke Ferdinand's army as it headed for Warsaw. Deciding to make a stand just south of the city, the Poles were defeated by the Austrians at the battle of Raszyn on 19 April. Despite a heroic effort, Poniatowski's army had to abandon Warsaw and retreat beyond Ferdinand's reach.

Perhaps as ominous as any of the other developments, Major Schill, a firebrand Prussian Hussar leader, gathered his men around him and begin a ride across northern Germany trying to raise a revolt against the French. Fortunately for Napoleon, Schill was largely ignored and his actions disavowed by the Prussian king. Still he had Jérome Bonaparte's kingdom of Westphalia in a state of confusion and near revolt. All these setbacks made Napoleon's victories all the more crucial, for if they had taken place without the Eckmühl campaign, they may have been the spark to bring Prussia into the war.

The pursuit of the Austrians

The initial pursuit of the Austrians south of the Danube was the responsibility of Marshal Bessieres. He commanded a combined force of cavalry and Bavarian infantry. Pursuing too rashly, part of his command was attacked and mauled at Neumarkt on 24 April. Bessieres halted and it was only the arrival of Marshal Lannes that the advance could resume. Another command, Marshal Masséna's, caught up with Hiller's men and,

Engraving of Archduke Charles de Habsbourg at the battle of Aspern. (Roger Viollet)

on 3 May, faced them across the Traun River at Ebelsberg.

Napoleon's camp before the battle of Ebelsberg. Many doubted that this costly little battle was necessary. (Painting by Antoine Pierre Mongin, Edimedia)

Masséna wanted to gain laurels by running down the retreating Austrians, so he quickly ordered an assault across the long bridge over the river. The French were pounded by batteries that had been positioned to maximize damage to anyone daring to cross. These were some of the best troops in Napoleon's army though, and they kept on coming. They broke into the town where they soon learned that most of Hiller's force had been hidden from view. Pinned by the withering fire, Masséna's men held on desperately to their foot-hold. More French crossed as their artillery swung into action to counter the Austrian batteries. The tremendous fire served to ignite the town, adding further horror to the ghastly carnage that sickened even the most hardened veterans. Pressing on through the smoke and flames, the French soldiers finally arrived at the castle on the hill above the town. There a vicious and heroic fight finally left the French in control of the castle and the town. Hiller broke off and retreated. While

ultimately victorious, Masséna's costly win was largely superfluous since Lannes had already outflanked Hiller's river line and would have dislodged them in a couple of hours without a fight. Masséna's men were too spent to launch an adequate pursuit and Hiller was able to retreat and cross the Danube largely unmolested.

Charles' army had escaped, but now Vienna was left exposed. Napoleon and his army had occupied the Habsburg capital on 12 May after only the smallest show of resistance by the home guard. The greatest triumph of the Viennese had been the destruction of the bridges over the Danube. At least they could comfort themselves that they had not been captured intact, as had happened in 1805.

As Napoleon's army advanced up the Danube toward Vienna, to the south events had also turned in the French favor. Eugene had sparred with John at Caldiero on

30 April, and the now outnumbered archduke had been forced into a retreat by a combination of pressure to his front and the collapsing situation on his northern flank.

The Austrian army of this era still depended on a large supply train, which slowed its advances and retreats. Many times Austrian commanders had to offer battle to protect the train, even when defeat seemed the most probable outcome. This was the situation John found himself in a little over a week later. At the Piave River John held his ground while Eugene assembled his army on the opposite bank. On the morning of 8 May, Eugene launched an assault across two fords. The leading forces established themselves and waited for more support. John had little in the way of options and sent his men forward to destroy the French on the northern bank. Eugene was ready for them and after repulsing the Austrian assaults, counterattacked and broke John's line in several places. By evening the victory was complete and Eugene had avenged his defeat at Sacile. Exploiting his advantage, Eugene advanced rapidly and pushed John's army out of Italy and towards Hungary. In a series of small actions, one after another of John's rearguards were overwhelmed, so that by 20 May, Eugene had reached Klagenfurt and was in a position to either join Napoleon or continue the pursuit of John.

While Eugene was following up the remnants of John's army, Marshal Lefebvre had reassembled his Bavarian Corps and set out to retake the Tyrol. With fire and sword the road to Innsbruck was cleared in a number of small actions. With the situation collapsing all around him, Chasteler began to retreat, leaving the Tyrolians to their fate. The Bavarians were too much to overcome and Innsbruck fell on 19 May. The Tyrol seemed pacified.

The Battle of Linz

As Napoleon advanced up the Danube, he left key crossing points guarded by corps-strength commands. At Linz the Wurttemberg Corps, under General Vandamme, was given just such a task. Vandamme was able to cross the Danube and create a *tête du pont* (a fortified bridgehead). This was a dagger pointed directly at the heart of Charles' army in Bohemia. In response, Charles sent General Kolowrat with the 3rd Corps to drive this incursion back over the river. The Austrian commander planned a three-pronged converging attack.

The Battle of Linz was a disjointed affair because the three Habsburg columns arrived and were repulsed one at a time. Furthermore, to disrupt Kolowrat's plan, Marshal Bernadotte, with elements of his Saxon Corps, arrived throughout the day. The result was complete failure on Kolowrat's part and his men retreated to lick their wounds. Napoleon's German allies had once more proved of great service, and for the time being Napoleon's supply line was secure.

From the Palace of Schönbrunn, Napoleon made plans for his next move. His line of supply was overextended, and while the line of the Danube was protected by the corps of Bernadotte, Vandamme, and Davout, his adversary was making no overtures toward peace. There were rumors of a British invasion, Archduke John's army could appear at almost any moment, and the Russians (French allies by treaty) appeared more menacing than reassuring. Since there was no word of any large formations near the river, Napoleon assumed that Charles and his army were somewhere near Brunn. French intelligence had completely broken down, for Charles was a few short miles away near Wagram.

Aspern-Essling

Napoleon planned and started the crossing of the Danube, first to Lobau Island, three-quarters of the way across, from where he could easily bridge the narrow channel to the northern (left) bank. He arranged several diversions, but Charles recognized them for what they were. From late on 18 May to

French infantry desperately trying to hold Essling from sustained Austrian attacks. (Myrbach, Roger-Viollet)

noon on 20 May, the French engineers worked to finish the pontoon bridges. Their work was badly hampered by the rising waters of the Danube, swollen by the melting snows of the Alps. Even so, the work was completed and two divisions of Masséna's Corps were hurried over to Lobau island. Molitor's division crossed over the further stream and occupied the towns of Aspern and Essling. Lasalle's light cavalry joined Molitor and took up a position between the two towns.

Masséna climbed to the top of the steeple of Aspern's church to view the surrounding countryside and look for signs of the Austrians. He spotted the campfires of the small reserve corps, but no others. Things seemed acceptably in order, so early on the morning of 21 May, he ordered the men of Boudet's and Legrand's divisions to the north bank in support of Molitor. Marshal Bessieres' cavalry crossed too and waited for the rest of the 4th Corps to arrive before expanding their perimeter. Carra St Cyr's division and Lannes' Corps were scheduled

to cross next, but a large barge crashed into and ruptured the bridge, preventing the crossing.

From a hill overlooking the river the Habsburgs were able to watch every development. Charles saw a golden opportunity: if he could interrupt the flow of men to the north bank of the river his massive army should be able to crush the force in front of him. To accomplish this goal, barges, logs, and toppled windmills were set alight and floated down the Danube. With the help of the high rushing waters, these makeshift rams smashed the bridge several times over the next two days. Each time the French sappers repaired it, the Austrians would send down another flaming ram.

With the flow of Napoleon's soldiers now interrupted, Charles closed in on Aspern and Essling with 100,000 men. At about 1.00 pm an alarmed messenger reported to Napoleon that a massive force of white-coated men was closing in on the French position. Napoleon sent an aide for confirmation, and learned that the number of the enemy was at least 80,000. He considered a withdrawal. Events were moving too fast for the French, for Charles had caught them ahead of plan.

The first to receive the brunt of Charles' attacks was Molitor's division, deployed in Aspern. The focal point of the Austrian attack was the church and cemetery on the west edge of town. Hiller's men came in before the two supporting corps could react, but advancing to the walls of the church they were hurled back by a tremendous fire. A second attempt, just before 3.00 pm, swept past the church into the town, but again was sent back as Molitor committed the last of his reserves. Hiller re-formed his men. By now the 1st and 2nd Corps were in position throughout the town. As their guns unlimbered and began to pound the French positions, Bessieres sent part of his cavalry to disrupt the fire and Charles countered with his own cavalry. In the swirling melee which followed, Charles fed in more regiments until the French cavalry withdrew.

By 4.30 pm a new assault has been launched from the three Habsburg columns aimed at Aspern. The church was once more the focal point and this time the bloodied French *fantassins* were expelled after a vicious hand-to-hand struggle. Much of the town was occupied and Napoleon's left flank was in danger of collapse. The Emperor sent Masséna forward with Legrand's division, to support Molitor's weary men. At bayonet point the Austrians were again thrown back.

The few guns the Emperor had were holding a critical portion of the line near Essling and providing covering fire to support the center between the two towns, so the Austrian cavalry had to be sent in once more on the left. This time they overran many of the French guns, but were halted by support infantry drawn up in massed formation behind the guns. Unable to break this formation, the Austrians flowed impotently around the infantry until driven back by the musketry. Their sacrifice had bought critical time but little else.

At 6.00 pm another attack was launched towards the town and was repelled. Charles himself rallied the repulsed troops and sent them in once more. This time they took the blazing town. The loss of this position spelled doom for Napoleon's army, so the Emperor sent in St Cyr's recently arrived division with the remnants of the two other previously decimated divisions to re-take Aspern. The spent Austrians were hurled back, rallied, and returned, but their impetus ran out half-way through the town and a French counter-attack had them slowly retreating. With stubborn defense they kept the strong-point of the church.

While the attacks were continuing around Aspern, Rosenberg's 4th Corps, divided into two columns, was moving into position. Without waiting for the supporting column, half of Rosenberg's men attacked. Waiting for them was Boudet's division under the direct command of Marshal Lannes. Boudet had arranged his men in the gardens and buildings that made up the village of Essling. The best fortification there was the granary, a massive structure with walls over three feet thick. Built at the end of the last century following riots caused by famine, it had been created with defense in mind. Boudet and a couple hundred of his best troops used it as a breakwater against the Austrian's assaults.

This strategy worked perfectly against the Habsburg first wave. It was easily repulsed and Lannes sent d'Espagne's heavy cavalry to run the fleeing enemy down. Many were caught from behind, but the pursuit was called off so that the metal-plated cavalrymen could respond to General Liechtenstein's counter-attacking cavalry. As the two forces closed on each other, General d'Espagne was killed by a round of canister. Deprived of their leader, the cuirassiers fought on, but, as would happen throughout the battle, the Austrian numbers proved decisive. However, the pursuing cavaliers were pulverized by the massed French artillery that Napoleon had placed in anticipation of such a reverse.

As night closed in on the village, the second half of Rosenberg's men were finally in position and came on. They took several of the outlying houses along with Essling's 'long garden'. Lannes was able to organize a force to storm these positions and soon all of

Often the infantry had little choice but to stand under artillery bombardment. (Sergent)

Essling was in French hands again. Marshal Lannes then held a meeting with Marshal Bessieres. The two men had detested each other since the Egyptian campaign of 1798, and Bessieres had been angered by Lannes' throughout the day, ordering Bessieres' cavalry to 'charge home.' The suggestion that he and his men had been hanging back was sufficient grounds for Bessieres to challenge his antagonist to a duel. The hot-headed Gascon was happy to accept, but Marshal Masséna came along and demanded both men put away their swords.

By nightfall, sporadic firing was all that remained of the day's combat. Essling was still in French hands, as was most of Aspern. Napoleon crossed the 2nd Corps and his Guard during the night and ordered Marshal Davout to prepare his men to cross too. Napoleon planned to take the initiative and break the Austrian center, using Lannes to attack with the newly arrived corps and the support of Bessieres' cavalry. Davout's men would exploit the success

and the Guard would be thrown in for the *coup de grâce*.

First Aspern would have to be re-taken again. Masséna, at the head of St Cyr's men, went over to the attack at 4.00 am. Driving the surprised Austrian occupants before them, they were halted by Austrian reserves coming up and were in turn driven back. The struggle continued, but by 7.00 am the town was in French hands once more.

While the fight had been going on around Aspern, Napoleon had sent Lasalle's light cavalry to attack south of Essling, so as to expand the deployment area and relieve any pressure coming from that direction. At first the fearsome cavalry had succeeded in driving back the opposing cavalry, but then they were stopped by the Austrian massed infantry. Not wishing to become the target of Rosenberg's many guns, Lasalle retired behind Essling toward the bridges, leaving Essling exposed. Rosenberg saw this as an invitation to seize the vital town once more. His men swept forward, but once again the two columns were not coordinated and met defeat.

Napoleon now sent Lannes forward, supported by the heavy cavalry. He was trying to repeat his victory of Austerlitz four years earlier by breaking the center and rolling up the two flanks. However, this time he was not using the crack troops of the camp of Boulogne but, with the exception of St Hilaire's men, new recruits. Even so, the attack went off well at first. Spearheaded once again by the ubiquitous 'Terrible 57th', the French smashed into the Froon Regiment (IR 54), captured one battalion, and sent the other two fleeing to the rear.

As the French came on, the Austrian artillery plowed great swaths through their ranks. This had to be stopped, so the French cavalry was committed against the Austrian guns. The cavalry came on brilliantly and quickly silenced the offending batteries. Breaking through, they encountered the infantry and cavalry of the center. The Austrian cavalry gave way, but the infantry stood firm and the French cavalry was forced to fall back. As it did so, on came Lannes' infantry.

Charles had watched developments and now committed his last available reserve in the area, the elite Grenadier Corps. They marched to fill the gap created by the wavering center, but they would still take critical minutes to arrive. Charles rode over

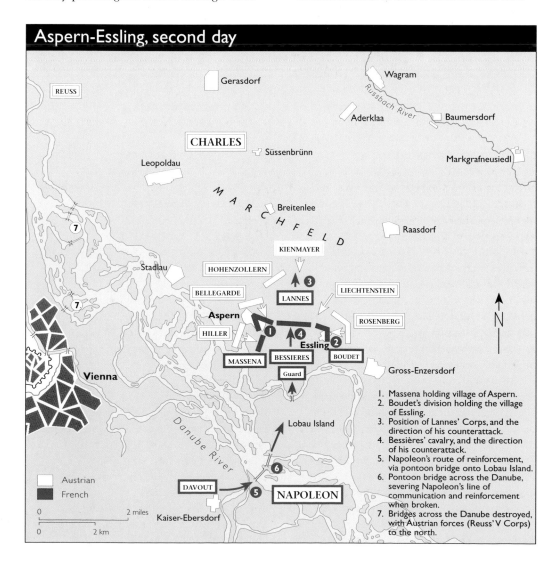

Aspern-Essling, second day

1. Massena holding village of Aspern.
2. Boudet's division holding the village of Essling.
3. Position of Lannes' Corps, and the direction of his counterattack.
4. Bessières' cavalry, and the direction of his counterattack.
5. Napoleon's route of reinforcement, via pontoon bridge onto Lobau Island.
6. Pontoon bridge across the Danube, severing Napoleon's line of communication and reinforcement when broken.
7. Bridges across the Danube destroyed, with Austrian forces (Reuss' V Corps) to the north.

to where his men were falling back and, grabbing the flag of the Zach Regiment (IR 15), rallied the men and led them back against the French. Lannes had now advanced almost a mile, but he received orders to call off the attack.

Austrian attempts to break the pontoon bridge had once again succeeded, this time using a floating mill set alight, and it might be a day before it could be restored. Worse, Davout's men had not managed to cross before the rupture, so Lannes' men represented the freshest fighting troops between Napoleon and annihilation. They had to be preserved.

Lannes' men held their position hoping for a quick repair of the lifeline. After confirming the disaster, Napoleon ordered the slow retreat of 2nd Corps. As the men fell they came under a devastating artillery barrage. General St Hilaire, perhaps the finest divisional general of France, had his left foot taken away by one of the rounds. The troops of the two conscript divisions began to leave the ranks in clumps and head to the rear, but Lannes remained calm and the line held. Finally they were back to their starting positions.

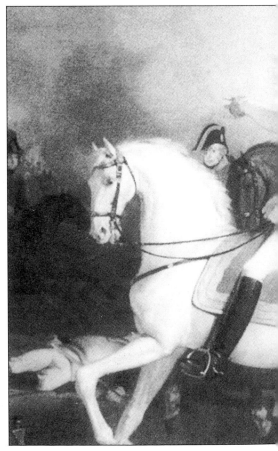

General Espagne was killed while leading one of the sacrificial charges of his cuirassiers.

With the crisis in the center averted, Charles once more sent forward attacks on the two towns. Aspern had changed hands twice already during Lannes' attack, and now the Habsburg's troops' effort was renewed. Charles had his howitzers converged into a single battery and set about pulverizing Aspern. The town once more ablaze, an assault took it but was again thrown back. Once more they came on, and by 1.00 pm Aspern was in Austrian hands for good. The defeated French set up a ring of fire to prevent any sallies from the town, but if Essling now fell, the artillery could be brought up to pound Napoleon into submission. Charles set about trying to make that happen.

Renewed attacks threw Boudet's men from all of Essling except the granary. There

Boudet remained with several elite companies, repelling all attempts to evict him. If the granary fell, all French hope would be lost. Charles sent in his elite grenadiers, but Boudet held on. Napoleon now sent in two battalions of Young Guard and one of the Middle Guard, under Mouton, to re-take Essling. The Guard came on and drove out the Austrians. Rosenberg committed more troops to surround the town and compel surrender. Napoleon responded by sending in General Rapp with two more battalions of Middle Guard to break out the beleaguered Guardsmen. Rapp, sizing up the situation, disobeyed the Emperor's orders

Archduke Charles with his staff in 1809. Years after rallying the Zach Infantry Regt he talked down the incident, saying 'You don't think a little fellow like me could carry one of those heavy flags, do you?' (Ian Castle)

and, rather than breaking off, defeated all comers. Charles had seen enough and ordered the attack on Essling discontinued.

With Napoleon pinned in Essling, the Austrians decided to decimate the French army using their superior number of guns. Almost 150 cannon began to pound the French center. Taking the brunt of the fire was 2nd Corps. Further behind them the battalions of the Old Guard had whole rows removed from their ranks under the incredible barrage. There was nowhere to go and the army was spent. Finally, Marshal Bessieres rallied some of the retreating men of the 2nd Corps and led them forward on foot as skirmishers to open fire upon the Austrian artillerists. The marshal's calm demeanor steadied the men and their fire took its toll upon their adversaries. However, by 4.00 pm Napoleon had returned to Lobau and accepted the inevitable. He would have to call off the battle and accept defeat. He left Marshal Lannes in command and began to organize the retreat, but soon after that Marshal Lannes was struck by a cannonball in the right kneecap, shattering his leg. He was carried to the rear past the Emperor, and as he was one of the small handful of Napoleon's personal friends, the Emperor wept openly upon seeing the wounded hero.

Charles was satisfied to let Napoleon retreat. His ammunition was low and his men were spent. During the night, the French evacuated to Lobau, where they spent a miserable night.

Napoleon licks his wounds

From a tactical point of view Aspern-Essling had been a draw, with both sides taking about the same casualties (22,000) but there was no mistaking the French strategic defeat. Napoleon did his best to disguise it, but the news spread throughout Europe, and the Allies hoped that perhaps now the 'ogre' could be brought down.

Following the battle, Napoleon made Lobau Island a massive fortified camp. He built sturdy bridges to bring over supplies and reinforcements, and he called up the reserves to strengthen the army. Bernadotte's Saxons arrived, and the forces from the Italian front – including Marmont's Dalmatian Corps – began their march to join him.

Napoleon had wanted Eugene to protect his southern (right) flank and had ordered him to move into position to accomplish this goal prior to the battle of Aspern-Essling. The importance of this move was doubled as a result of the defeat. As Eugene moved north with his troops, he caught General Jellacic retreating from the Tyrol to link up with Archduke John in Hungary. At the battle of St Michael on 25 May, the badly outnumbered Austrians were mauled and very few of Jellacic's men made it to Hungary. Soon these regulars would be sorely missed.

The victory removed any immediate threat to Napoleon's strategic right flank, and Eugene was now free to pursue Archduke John and attempt to annihilate him before he could join Charles north of the Danube. John had divided his army after his defeat at the Piave River. One force remained under his command, while the other, under Gyulai, was to defend the Habsburg province of Carinthia against Macdonald's wing of Eugene's army, which now operated independently. Supporting Macdonald's efforts was the force of Marmont.

Marmont had fallen back to Zara on the Adriatic coast following his defeat on 15 April and had gathered his troops together for a counterattack. He struck on 13 May at Mt Kitta, initiating a series of actions that destroyed Stoichewich's division. He was aided in no small part by the huge number of guns he had assembled – 78 in all. Marmont had come up through the artillery, as had Napoleon, and he was regarded as the premier artillery specialist under the French emperor.

Following the defeat of Stoichewich, Marmont set off in the direction of Vienna. His first goal was to link up with Macdonald, one of whose divisions was besieging the citadel at Graz. Unknown to Marmont, Gyulai had made a relief effort and the

French had retreated rather than face a two-front battle. As a result Marmont's leading element marched on Graz unaware that the town was no longer in French hands. The 84th Line, two battalions strong, advanced against Graz and, after recovering from the shock of being fired upon, threw out the advance guard of Gyulai. Taking up a position in a church and its cemetery, they repelled attacks by an entire division before finally cutting their way out of their encircled position when their ammunition gave out.

Marmont's main force soon came up and Graz was retaken from the weary defenders. The 84th Line's legendary defense earned them the motto '*Un contre dix*,' (One against ten), which was later inscribed upon their eagle. Following Graz, Marmont and Macdonald marched to join Napoleon's army on Lobau.

While Marmont was heading north, Eugene had caught John near Raab. John had been reinforced by the Insurrection, the Hungarian militia, but was still outnumbered and outclassed. He had chosen a strong position, however and felt confident of his line of retreat. The Battle of Raab, fought on 14 June, was a vicious little battle in which the Habsburgs initially made good use of the terrain and inflicted losses upon Eugene's men. Then the tables turned and the Austrians got the worst of it. Once the stronghold of the Kis-Meyer farm had fallen for good, all hope of victory was lost to John

Tyrolian insurgents revolt against Napoleon. Despite many victories over Bavarian and French troops, eventually Napoleon's victories on the Danube left them exposed and alone (Painting by Franz von Defregger, Roger-Viollet)

and he called a retreat. John's army had suffered twice the losses of Eugene's but had fought well enough for no effective pursuit to take place. His army retreated to the north bank of the Danube and established contact with Charles' army. Eugene and his men joined Napoleon.

To the north, Prince Poniatowski was leading the Polish forces to victory. After losing Warsaw, he had appeared to melt into the countryside but had reassembled behind Ferdinand's line of communication and incited the Austrian (formerly Polish) province of Galicia to rise in revolt. The Austrian situation grew steadily worse but they were given a reprieve by the Poles' Russian 'allies,' who so devastated the areas they operated in that Poniatowski had to dispatch large parts of his army to protect his own people from their 'friends.' There was no question though, that given time, Charles would have to watch his northern flank as well as his southern.

The stage was now almost set for Napoleon to attempt another attack on Charles. He called up Wrede's Bavarian division, but could not bring up any more Bavarian troops, because the Tyrol had once more exploded in revolt. Innsbruck had again fallen to the Tyrolian insurgents and raids were being made into the Danube valley in an attempt to break the French line of communication. This problem would not be solved until the Austrians were knocked out of the war.

As Charles waited for the hammer blow he was sure would come, he looked to the west for help. Britain had promised the Habsburgs a raid in force on Germany. This plan had evolved into an attack on Antwerp, now the major French naval arsenal, which was much more to London's liking. To accomplish this goal, a huge armada had been assembled and supplies gathered – a force that Wellington would have envied. However, May became June and June became July with no sign of the British. Intelligence was such that there was no doubt of the invasion coming, but when it would happen was unknown even to Parliament. Napoleon made what provision he could to repel an

attack, and then carried on with his plans for Charles.

Wagram

Lobau had become a huge warehouse. By the day of the battle the army had grown to 190,000 men. Charles had only 140,000 to oppose them. Napoleon had retaken his former *tête de pont* on the north bank and it was from there that Charles expected the attack to come. However, Napoleon was planning to drop bridges from the east edge of the island and swing around the Austrian positions from the south and east. Then in a huge wheeling motion, he would drive the Austrians away from the Danube and bring over the remainder of his army from the now undefended *tête du pont*. He put this plan into effect on the morning of 5 July 1809.

Under cover of a violent thunderstorm, the French constructed the bridges needed to transport the corps of Davout, Masséna, and Oudinot. The Austrian skirmish line was driven off or captured and the crossing took place with only light opposition. Marshal Berthier, when issuing the orders to the corps, had accidentally given the same crossing to two corps. This caused a several hour delay to sort out the traffic jam, but finally all three corps were across. Deploying on an east-west axis the French drove all enemies before them. Supporting these efforts, Napoleon opened up a terrific bombardment from his prepared positions on Lobau.

All was going well for Napoleon. Instead of finding the main Austrian army in positions around Aspern-Essling, all he faced was the outpost divisions of Nordmann and Klenau. The main Habsburg army was positioned five miles away, centered on the village of Wagram. The few battered troops to deal with the French onslaught were driven back and by noon all enemies opposite Lobau were gone. By this time, Bernadotte's Saxon Corps had joined the other three and they began an advance over the *Marchfeld* towards the main Austrian

After the failure of the bridges over the Danube during the battle of Aspern-Essling, Napoleon did not intend to be dangerously exposed again. He supervised the bridge building himself before the battle of Wagram. (Myrbach, Musee de l'armee)

position, with more French and Allied troops entering the plain from the Lobau bridges.

Charles had sent a message to his brother John to move from his positions near Pressburg and hurry to the battlefield, but John's men were scattered along the Danube and he failed to appreciate the urgency of Charles' request. It would be early the next morning before he would get his force on the road. While John dawdled, Charles and Emperor Francis watched the French advance with increasing trepidation.

As the four leading corps fanned out over the *Marchfeld*, the heavy cavalry positioned on the Austrian right tried to disrupt the advance by charging the Saxon cavalry opposite them. Although initially successful, they were soon driven back by the lighter Saxon horse. It had been a brave attempt by the Austrians, but they had had the misfortune to face the finest line cavalry in the world. There would be no further attempts to stop Napoleon's deployment.

It was now approaching evening and Napoleon decided to try to exploit the gains made during the day. Ever fearful that his adversary would slip away during the night, he ordered an assault along the line. His mistake would be a lack of effective effort to coordinate the several corps.

At about 7.00 pm Oudinot's Corps, with the support of Dupas' small division from Bernadotte's Corps, attacked the center of the enemy line. The defense was centered around Baumersdorf. Spearheading the assault was Grandjean's division, the best in the army apart from the Guard. The 'Terrible 57th' Line attacked the southern end of the village and drove out two regiments facing it, capturing many Austrians. They continued over the little Russbach stream and into the northern half of the town. Here their furious attack ran out of steam, for Hardegg's men dug in and would not budge. The Austrians knew that if the town was taken, their position would be hopelessly compromised. Both sides laid down a withering fire and casualties mounted.

While this action was taking place, the 10th Legere had crossed the marshy stream and had begun to climb the slopes beyond. Charles was there and knew that if the heights were taken, Baumersdorf would be quickly surrounded and would certainly fall. He ordered one of his cavalry regiments, the Vincent Chevaulegers, to charge. Here was a fight between one of the best cavalry regiments in the Habsburg army and one of the best French infantry regiments. The first round went to the French and the cavalry recoiled. Charles regrouped them and they came on again, only to suffer the same result. While the 10th Legere repulsed the charges, their progress was temporarily halted. They waited for two more divisions of Oudinot's Corps to come up on their flank. These two divisions were made up of the conscripts of the 4th battalions. They had little stomach for the murderous artillery barrage that was pouring down on them. After a brief attempt to advance they halted, then fell back.

The retreat of Oudinot's two divisions left Grandjean's men isolated. It was at this moment that Charles turned to the twice-repulsed Vincent Chevaulegers and said: 'It is clear that you are no longer Latour's dragoons.' This was a reference to their heroic past. Stung by the reproach, the regiment charged once more, with the corps commander, Hohenzollern, leading. The 10th could no longer hold on. They fell back, firing as they went, and were driven across the stream. The repulse of the 10th Legere left the flanks of the 57th Line open to attack, so they too had to retire. The French assault in the center was over, with nothing to show for it.

To the left of this action the elements of the army of Italy now attempted to assault the Russbach heights. Led by General Macdonald, three divisions crossed the stream and attacked. Pressing uphill against the Austrian gun line, they were on the verge of breaking through when fresh Habsburg reserves counterattacked. Macdonald's men recoiled down the slope but regrouped and were beginning a fresh advance when the Vincent Chevaulegers attacked from the right flank. The heroic cavalry unit had rallied from their assault on the 10th Legere and, seeing the opportunity, charged. Seras' division gave way and routed to the rear. While Macdonald's right flank was collapsing, his left was doing no better. General Dupas' division had crossed the Russbach and had become mired in the swampy ground. Finally extricating themselves, they made a first assault up the slopes. The Austrian fire drove them back, and as they retreated, Macdonald's reserves mistook the white-coated Saxons attached to Dupas as Austrians and opened fire. Since it was Italian troops initiating the fire, they too were clad in white and the Saxons returned fire. Before the generals could restore the situation, the Italians had been badly shaken and the hapless Saxons had completely dispersed. When the panic caused by the situation on its right flank rippled down the line, the entire army of Italy dissolved into a rout. A disconsolate Eugene was comforted by Macdonald with the words that the attack had been ill-considered and that Napoleon would soon realize it. He did.

With half of his small division destroyed, Dupas could not hold on for long. Soon his men began to flee to the rear. As they headed back, they were passed by a brigade of Saxons aiming to take Wagram. It was now nearly 8.00 pm and Bernadotte had sent forward his three remaining infantry brigades one at a time. Napoleon had realized that if the Saxon attack was to have any hope of success, it had to have artillery support, so he deployed the horse artillery of the Guard and the Saxon and Bavarian batteries to pulverize Wagram. The effect was

Wagram, second day

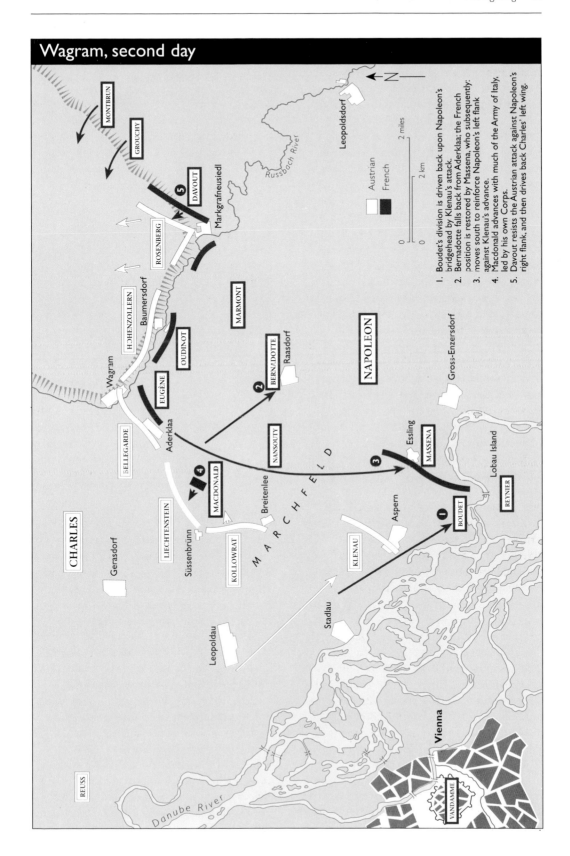

1. Boudet's division is driven back upon Napoleon's bridgehead by Klenau's attack.
2. Bernadotte falls back from Aderklaa; the French position is restored by Massena, who subsequently moves south to reinforce Napoleon's left flank against Klenau's advance.
3.
4. Macdonald advances with much of the Army of Italy, led by his own Corps.
5. Davout resists the Austrian attack against Napoleon's right flank, and then drives back Charles' left wing.

Austrian
French

0   2 miles
0   2 km

N

MONTBRUN

GROUCHY

DAVOUT

Markgrafneusiedl

ROSENBERG

Baumersdorf

HOHENZOLLERN

MARMONT

Wagram

OUDINOT

EUGÈNE

Aderklaa

BELLEGARDE

CHARLES

Gerasdorf

LIECHTENSTEIN

Süssenbrünn

MACDONALD

KOLLOWRAT

Breitenlee

M A R C H F E L D

BERNADOTTE

Raasdorf

NANSOUTY

NAPOLEON

Essling

MASSENA

Gross-Enzersdorf

Lobau Island

REYNIER

Aspern

BOUDET

KLENAU

Stadlau

Leopoldau

REUSS

Vienna

VANDAMME

Danube River

Russbach River

Leopoldsdorf

devastating and allowed the single Saxon brigade to gain a foothold in the town. Caught in a fierce firefight, the outnumbered Saxons held on until the next brigade came up. These men penetrated to the other side of Wagram but a counterattack threw them back. Retreating through the gloom and smoke, they fell back to the third and final brigade of Bernadotte's troops which had finally entered the battle. Once more, the Saxons were mistaken for Austrians and were fired upon by their own side. With fire from friend and foe alike, their morale collapsed and they fled. This rout started a general panic and soon all hard-won gains were gone. The panicking infantry fell back toward Aderklaa under the protection of their cavalry and guns. This attack had been as dismal a failure as the others.

As Bernadotte's men had stepped off on their attack, Davout on the far French right had crossed the Russbach and had met stiff resistance. Aware that darkness would make coordination of any attack impossible, Davout wisely called it off and retreated to his starting position.

The first day ended with the French army unnerved by the mauling they had received. They were, though, firmly on the *Marchfeld* and still under their Emperor. During the night, Charles surveyed the situation. Things had gone well, but it was too late to change the orders for the next day. These called for a double envelopment attack on the French. He had a sizable force that could attack on his right, but unless Archduke John arrived soon, his left attack stood no chance. Napoleon planned for Davout on his right to be the main attack, and for his other corps to be committed as Davout's attack developed.

Napoleon felt confident that with Aderklaa held and several corps in reserve, ready to fill any gaps that might develop, his plan could succeed. What he did not know was that Bernadotte had pulled out of Aderklaa at 3.00 am and fallen back a thousand yards. While it was true that the Saxon Corps had been roughly treated, to pull out of such a key position was to invite disaster. Bernadotte felt his men had been

One of the finest French generals, André Masséna. Wagram was his last victory, and owed much to his performance, though he was confined to his carriage by a previous wound. (Ann Ronan Picture Library)

mistreated and deserved reinforcements which had not come. Telling anyone who would listen that he could have turned the Austrians out of their position by a 'telling maneuver,' he would earn Napoleon's wrath the following day when these words reached the Emperor's ears.

The morning of 6 July 1809 broke hot and sweltering. Several of Charles' corps had been on the march since the early hours. The key to Charles' attack was to turn both of the French flanks and drive to the bridgehead at Lobau. There he could cut off the French retreat and hopefully induce panic in the enemy. The main attack on the French left would be spearheaded by Klenau's 6th Corps, with the support of Kolowrat's 3rd Corps. Charles further hoped that John would appear on the French right

Portrait of General Macdonald. He wore his old Revolutionary War uniform for Wagram, emphasizing that he had only just been rehabilitated after a long period of disgrace. After the battle he was compensated with the award of a marshal's baton.

and close the trap from that direction. To support this he ordered Rosenberg's 4th Corps to attack Davout's 3rd Corps. John's arrival would fall on Davout's flank and seal the victory.

Klenau's initial cannonade broke the morning stillness at about 4.00 am. Facing them initially was Boudet's single division of Masséna's 4th Corps. Seeing the attack begin, Masséna sent Legrand's division to aid Boudet. They would face the full wrath of Kolowrat's men. Badly outnumbered Legrand's division stood for a brief time before being overwhelmed, and a hole several miles wide was opened in the French line.

While this was taking place, Boudet's men were grimly holding on to the charred ruins of Aspern. Supporting their defense were two batteries of guns, which poured fire into the powerful tide of white-coated Austrians. When Legrand's division gave way and the French line was breached, Austrian cavalry flooded into the gap, circled around the northern flank of Boudet, and came charging down his flank and rear. The exposed

gunners were sabered and when an infantry regiment went into the plain to rescue the artillery, it too was cut up. At the same time the left flank of Boudet was turned and soon almost all of his division panicked and broke for the rear. A brief stand was made at Essling, but there was to be no repetition of the hotly contested fighting of two months earlier. Essling was soon clear of the French. It was only as Klenau's men approached the *tête de pont* that the vast number of guns left on the island stopped the pursuit. The first half of Charles' plan had been achieved, but Klenau had no support, for Kolowrat had stopped his advance and was lending lukewarm support to the action developing around Aderklaa. Further there was no sign of a closing pincer coming from the other flank.

Rosenberg had made a good start. His attack has surprised Davout's men and sent the outposts streaming to the rear in panic. However, once stability had returned to the French ranks, the attack petered out and quiet fell in that part of the field.

Napoleon had intended the attack by Davout to be a decisive blow. While the Austrian attack had failed to drive Davout from his position, it had cost the French in the area much of their ammunition. It would now take several hours of re-supply and prepare for the planned attack. Perhaps more important was that news of Rosenberg's attack caused Napoleon to shift his reserves to the French right, away from the area where later it would be needed most.

The village of Aderklaa was a key position on the battlefield and both commanders recognized this. Charles had ordered his I Corps under Bellegarde to attack and take the village. Napoleon believed that the Saxon Corps under Bernadotte was still in possession of Aderklaa and he sent most of Masséna's Corps to support them, but Bernadotte had pulled his battered men from the position as he felt that it was too exposed to the tremendous artillery concentration in the area. That danger was real enough, but the loss of this key position posed an even greater threat.

Bellegarde's troops were able to take the village with few losses and began to dig in. When Napoleon returned from his ride to Davout's position, he ordered Bernadotte's men to retake Aderklaa. The Saxons came on but were devastated by the Habsburg guns that the marshal had so feared the night before. Soon the shaken men gave way and fled to the rear. Bernadotte was carried along with them, frantically trying to rally his men, with little effect, when he came into the Emperor's presence. Napoleon shook his head and asked if this was the 'telling maneuver' of which Bernadotte had spoken. The marshal had little

time to wallow in this humiliation, however, as the Saxon infantry retreat continued for some time.

In truth much of the French left had effectively ceased to exist. The only organized force was some cavalry and the remaining two divisions of Masséna's 4th Corps. These were now sent to attack Aderklaa. Carra St Cyr's division went into the attack to Masséna's call to 'throw out that *merde.*' The men came on through a hail of cannon shot and at the points of their bayonets ejected the Austrians from the houses. Following up their victory, St Cyr's

Napoleon snatching a moment's rest on the battlefield of Wagram, his staff and household at work around him. (Edimedia)

burning village. Yard by yard, Aderklaa fell into Molitor's hands, despite several attempts to reclaim it for the Habsburgs. It was just past 9.00 am and the battle hung in the balance.

As Napoleon's reserves made their way back from their march to the right flank, Charles organized a massive assault against Aderklaa. He committed his 1st Reserve Corps of elite grenadiers to support the efforts of Bellegarde's attack from the north and Kolowrat's from the south. This attack came after a two-hour pounding from over 100 Austrian guns. Seeing that their retreat would soon be cut off and down to almost half their number, Molitor's troops evacuated the village, firing as they went. Unlike the Saxons, however, they remained a cohesive force.

Napoleon now needed to buy some time. With Davout's attack at last underway, Napoleon needed to hold his front long enough to allow Davout to win the battle. His first concern was to deal with the threat to his rear from Klenau, so he sent the remains of Masséna's Corps south. He then ordered much of his center to swing to the west and align themselves to face the advancing troops under Kolowrat and Liechtenstein's reserve grenadiers. This maneuver would take over an hour. To buy this time, Napoleon sent in his heavy cavalry under Nansouty. The 4,000 cuirassiers and carabineers swept across the open plain. The Austrian cannon rounds plowed the earth around them and tore holes through their ranks, but the cavalry came on, and after crushing one battalion, dashed themselves upon the grenadier squares. Here they had no effect. They swung around the squares and charged the Austrian gun line from the flank. Before they could do much good, however, they were themselves charged in the flank by Austrian cavalry which had hurried up. The melee was brief, and soon the remaining French horse were flying back

men carried on past the village. They had gone beyond their effective support and were counterattacked so successfully that two of their 'sacred' eagles were lost. Charles had been on the spot to rally his retreating men and led them forward to retake Aderklaa. Charles was wounded in the conflict, taking a bullet in the shoulder.

As St Cyr's men reeled back from the fighting, Masséna sent in his last reserve, Molitor's division. These were the men who had held on to Aspern against all odds in May. They first repelled a vicious cavalry attack, then fell upon the defenders of the to the safety of their lines. The charge had done little more than stall the Austrians.

While the cavalry was creating this costly diversion, Napoleon ordered a massive battery to be formed opposite Rosenberg's men. Made up mostly of Imperial Guard artillery, it had 112 guns and was commanded by General Lauriston. Galloping into position under a hail of fire from the Austrian guns, the grand battery set up and began to bombard the luckless 3rd Corps. This was the largest concentration of artillery ever assembled during a field battle and its effect was devastating. First Kolowrat's guns were silenced, then the massed Austrian infantry was targeted. The solid rounds tore through the Austrian formations, taking out entire files with a single shot. To add to these horrors, the dry grass ignited and many of the wounded on both sides were burned alive. Several times the Austrians tried to dislodge the guns, but they were pulverized before they could have any real effect. The tide was finally turning in Napoleon's favor.

Davout had prepared his attack against Markgrafneusiedl, the linchpin of the Austrian left, with a heavy artillery bombardment. After pounding much of the village into rubble and setting many of the buildings alight, Davout sent forward his four divisions. Those under Morand and Friant swung to the right of the village, while the other two, under Puthod and Gudin, went straight in. Morand and Friant advanced in echelon to the right and hit the back of the village. The leading troops were stopped and the Austrian general Nordmann saw an opportunity to turn Morand's flank. Driving off one regiment with his attack, Nordmann was in turn hit in the flank by Friant's men. In the fighting Nordmann was killed, and soon his men were running to the rear.

Markgrafneusiedl was still in Austrian hands though, and the divisions of Puthod and Gudin were making slow progress. In desperate house-to-house fighting Davout's men eventually evicted Rosenberg's men. The fighting continued past the village to the medieval tower above. This was taken

and retaken several times until it was finally in French hands.

It was now around noon and the wounded Charles arrived with fresh troops to stem the French tide. His cavalry was able to repel the first assault, but was finally overwhelmed by superior numbers. The whole of the Austrian line on the Russbach heights began to give way and retreat to the west.

When Napoleon received the news of the capture of Markgrafneusiedl, he assumed, correctly, that any enemy reserves were being sent in that direction to try to stop Davout. Knowing that the Habsburg line was stretched to breaking point, he launched General Macdonald's three small divisions at the Austrian center. Macdonald formed his men into a huge square and began the advance. Supported by Wrede's Bavarian division on his right, the huge phalanx lumbered forward. The remaining Austrian guns turned all available fire upon them. It was impossible to miss a target of this size, and Macdonald's men paid a fearful price. On they came, nevertheless, and soon the devastated Austrian line began to yield. A hole was created, but soon closed because there were no cavalry to exploit the victory. With the Guard cavalry commander, Marshal Bessieres, badly wounded in Nansouty's earlier attack, the orders to bring on the Guard cavalry were never executed. Isolated, Macdonald's men had to finally give way and fall back the way they had come. The moment passed and the complete victory slipped away.

In the south, Masséna had evicted Klenau's men from Essling and Aspern and Klenau was now in full retreat, having come within a hair of winning the day, but having received no support.

Victory was in the capable hands of Davout and he was making the most of it. Austrians in one position after another on the Russbach heights had to turn and face his flanking attack, while the French opposite these positions added their weight to the onslaught. These were Oudinot's 2nd Corps and Marmont's Corps. The pressure from two sides was too much and Charles ordered a retreat toward Bohemia. By 2.00 pm the field was in French hands, but the decimated French-Allied army had no appetite for pursuit. Once the victory was assured, many men collapsed in place and rested.

It was about 4.00 pm when Archduke John's first troops arrived on the field. Besides scaring some understandably skittish Saxons, he could do no good. After sizing up the situation, he too ordered a retreat to Bohemia.

The cost of the fighting

Losses on both sides were staggering, approximately 40,000 killed, wounded and missing from each army. Among the upper ranks losses had been equally devastating. The French lost five generals killed and 38 wounded. The Austrians, less apt to lead from the front, still had four generals killed and 13 wounded. As a result of the battle, Napoleon honored three generals on the battlefield. He made Oudinot, Marmont, and Macdonald into marshals. Bernadotte was dismissed from command after he issued a letter of congratulation to the Saxons, giving them great credit in the preceding day's battle. This was the Emperor's purview and Bernadotte had once more overstepped his authority. The act was particularly galling given that his withdrawal from Aderklaa had cost the French so dearly, but his earlier comments had not been forgotten either.

The following day the French reorganized their army while Charles retreated toward Znaim. Marmont's Corps caught up with the Austrians on the evening of 10 July and tried to pin the Habsburgs before they could retreat across the Thaya River. Though he took heavy losses, Marmont succeeded in pinning much of the army until Napoleon showed with reinforcements. The battle was in full progress the following day when an Austrian rode out between the lines with an armistice request. Many French veterans wept at the thought of their old enemy

escaping once more with a punitive peace treaty.

Napoleon met with Liechtenstein and a one-month truce was signed. Napoleon needed the rest to recoup from this bloody campaign, as did the Austrians. The latter hoped though that they could gain some leverage from the now imminently expected British invasion of the Dutch coast.

After months of dithering, the British force finally set sail in the last week of July 1809. Their object was the port of Antwerp and its naval base, but first the British had to take the island of Walcheren. Located at the mouth of the Scheldt River, they needed the island as a base of operations from which to launch the attack on Antwerp. The army, under the Earl of Chatham, was the strongest Britain could muster and the naval support enormous.

A 20,000-strong force landed on the island and advanced on Flushing. Defending this fortified town was a rag-tag force under General Monnet. While delays allowed the French to send over more troops, the final outcome seemed predetermined. Monnet flooded the island, which is mostly below sea level, delaying the British advance, but when the massive fleet ran the French fort at the mouth of the Scheldt, the British bombardment secured the outcome. On 15 August, the French asked for surrender terms.

Chatham's victory was in vain, for he took far too long organizing his force to push up the Scheldt for Antwerp. Probes were made in several directions, but no firm decision was taken about which path to take. Meanwhile Bernadotte had been appointed to take over command of the district defenses. Sensing that this was perhaps his last chance to recover his reputation, Bernadotte pitched in and organized his forces so that every British attempt was frustrated.

As continued attempts were made to seek a weak spot in the French defenses, a virulent fever broke out in the British army. The marshy ground of Walcheren was a perfect breeding ground for mosquitoes and soon 100 men were dying each day. After more than a month of terrible losses the British gave up and set sail for home. There recriminations waited for all the leaders involved.

In the Tyrol, Napoleon sent in troops in such numbers that the outcome was no longer in doubt The rebels were suppressed one band at a time. Finally, Andreas Hofer was captured and sent to his trial and martyrdom. After that, all rebellion was quelled.

As the months dragged on, Napoleon waited for the negotiations in the Viennese Palace of Schönbrunn to reach a conclusion. There he put on parades and entertained his Austrian counterparts. He even had time to re-visit the battlefield of Austerlitz, scene of his greatest triumph. Once the Walcheren expedition had failed, it was merely a matter of working out the details of the penalty to be suffered by the Habsburgs for their violation of peace and their alliance with the hated British.

It was during one of many reviews at this time that General Rapp noticed a young man acting suspiciously. Searching him he found a large knife. The young Saxon, Friedrich Stapps, soon confessed to planning to assassinate Napoleon. Brought before the Emperor, he explained that the reason for his plan was to liberate his subject country. Napoleon offered clemency for an apology, but Stapps refused. His plot and subsequent execution deeply troubled Napoleon. This was the tip of the iceberg, a symptom of growing German nationalism. The French Revolution had spread the modern ideas of liberty, but the young men of Europe did not necessarily believe that it should happen under French rule. However, these were specters of the future: for the time being, there was peace to be settled.

Heading up the negotiations for Francis was Prince Metternich. He had the same goal as Charles, the preservation of the Habsburg Empire. Promising peace and friendship, he succeeded in fooling Napoleon into making more modest demands for peace than he could have exacted. Napoleon received

Carinthia, Carniola, and the Adriatic ports; part of Galicia was regained by the Poles; the Salzburg area of the Tyrol was given to the Bavarians; and the small Tarnopol area was given to the treacherous Russians. However, most of the hereditary lands remained with Francis' crown.

Napoleon made the critical error of believing that a permanent peace with the great monarchies of Europe was possible. Austria, Russia, and Prussia believed that peace should only be made in order to regain lost strength, but that ultimately the 'Corsican usurper' had to be removed. It would have been better for Napoleon had he dismantled the Habsburg holdings, perhaps giving Bohemia to Bavaria or Saxony, making Hungary independent, and leaving the Habsburgs with Austria alone. This arrangement would have left Austria in no position to turn against him, as they would do four years later. Metternich understood all this, and directed negotiations towards a more moderate conclusion.

A false peace

The year 1809 had been difficult for Emperor Napoleon. He had withstood threats on every front. When peace was finally signed, on 14 October 1809 at the Schönbrunn palace, Napoleon was already planning to take the Austrian princess Marie-Louise as his new wife. Josephine could no longer bear children, and Napoleon believed that a son and heir was needed to continue the regime. Originally, Napoleon had approached Tsar Alexander with the idea of marrying his sister Catherine, but because the dowager empress rejected the idea of a family alliance with heretic France, or because of a possible incestuous relationship with her, Alexander had spurned the offer. He quickly married off Catherine to the Prince of Oldenburg and kept her at close quarters. The offer to marry the younger sister Anne was put off until she was older.

Napoleon was no fool and knew he had been rejected a second time. So when peace

One of the greatest armadas Britain had ever seen bombarding the fortress of Flushing on the Dutch coast. (National Maritime Museum)

came with Austria, he turned his attention to creating an alliance with them instead. Metternich could not have been happier, as this sacrifice assured that Napoleon turned his eyes away from the Habsburgs. Married by proxy, the princess was brought to France where Napoleon met her near Compiegne and hosted the bridal party prior to the formal church wedding held in the Louvre. While the marriage was hailed as a harbinger of peace for Europe, many of Napoleon's men felt that the ideals of the Revolution were being lost and that their good luck charm, Josephine, had been discarded.

Josephine went to Malmaison where she lived out most of her remaining life. Napoleon saw her little, for Marie-Louise resented the continuing friendship. Napoleon clearly loved his new bride and she him. He became much more domestic and housebound, and the pace of his previous frenetic activity slackened. The war in Spain was not going as well as it should, but he never managed to pull himself away from his bride long enough to take the field in Spain again.

The new empress fulfilled her part in the bargain as she was soon pregnant. It was on 19 March 1811 that the King of Rome, Napoleon II, was born.

The war with Russia, 1812

Causes

While Napoleon and his new bride visited sights around his empire in 1810 and 1811, the relationship with Russia was deteriorating. Tsar Alexander had been under pressure ever since Tilsit in 1807 to break the restrictions on trade that the treaty had imposed. His first response was to permit open smuggling, but this was soon decried by the French and he looked for another answer.

Napoleon was well aware of Alexander's duplicity. The rejection of Napoleon's marriage proposal and the lackluster performance of the Russians in 1809 had irritated Napoleon so much that he struck back by incorporating large parts of Germany and the Balkans into the French empire. Included in this was the Duchy of Oldenburg, whose ruler had just married into the Tsar's family.

Alexander resented these actions intensely. He was even affronted by Napoleon's marriage to an Austrian princess. He declared in December of 1810 that he would no longer refuse to trade with neutrals

Napoleon had difficulty in believing that Alexander wanted war, but he prepared to assemble his army in Poland to deal with the errant ally. Napoleon approached the Swedes with the prospect of regaining Finland should they join the war effort. Bernadotte had become the Swedish crown prince and *de facto* ruler, and he was more than willing to listen to these proposals, but the French ambassador in Stockholm became incensed that Sweden continued to trade with neutrals and broke off relations. Bernadotte went to Tsar Alexander looking for a better deal. He was offered Norway, a Danish possession, for his cooperation. Bernadotte accepted and turned his back on his homeland. Alexander would find that Bernadotte was as unreliable an ally in 1812 as he had been a marshal for Napoleon.

Russia wanted war by the beginning of 1811 and was making plans to invade Poland. Only poor finances made this impossible. A signal success in Turkey led to a peace that released Russian troops in the south for use against Napoleon. Alexander had a million men under arms by 1812, but they were scattered throughout the vast Russian territories. It took enormous time to mobilize them, but this had some advantages for the Tsar.

In Paris a spy ring had been discovered, which particularly embarrassed Napoleon. One of the key players was Alexander Tchernishev, a Russian colonel who had made friends with Napoleon. The Emperor was particularly chagrined to discover, after the Russian's return to Moscow, that a worker in the French Ministry of War had been handing over to the spy every return of the troops in the field. When this was announced, it was treated as proof of Russia's bad faith.

Napoleon had his own successes. The French Foreign Minister Champigny showed a forged document to the King of Prussia indicating that the Tsar proposed the elimination of Prussia in the near future. This threw the King into France's arms and he provided a corps for the war effort against Russia. Austria was equally compliant. When promised that they would be able to keep their existing territories if they contributed 30,000 men, they quickly agreed.

Napoleon had received repeated warnings that to invade Russia could be disastrous, particularly from Caulaincourt, his recent ambassador to St Petersburg. But Caulaincourt had been fooled before by Alexander's protestations. Napoleon assumed that threats of war to the death should the Russian borders be violated were nothing more than bluster. What Napoleon did not know was that the vacillating Tsar had experienced a mystical vision in which he saw himself as God's shield against the Antichrist Napoleon. This gave the barely-sane Tsar a new resolve.

By August 1811 Napoleon had accepted that war was inevitable. He began to plan for the campaign the following year, with 600,000 men beginning their march to the borders of Russia, with few knowing their final destination.

Napoleon enters Russia

The French-Allied invasion force designated for the campaign was divided into five commands. The three central armies were commanded by Napoleon, his brother Jérôme, who was King of Westphalia, and his stepson Eugene Beauharnais, Viceroy of Italy. One of the two flanking armies, the southern, was commanded by the Austrian Prince Schwarzenberg, while Marshal Macdonald led a combined French and Prussian corps. Napoleon's main force was made up of the Guard, Davout's 1st Corps, Ney's 3rd Corps, and two reserve cavalry corps under Montbrun, and Nansouty. On his right Jérôme had Poniatowski's (Polish) 5th Corps, Vandamme's (Westphalian)

8th Corps, and Reynier's (Saxon) 7th Corps, plus a cavalry corps under Latour-Maubourg. Eugene commanded his own 4th Corps, the 6th Corps under St Cyr, and a cavalry corps under Grouchy. In all, the central forces totaled some 320,000 men. The central army began to cross the River Niemen early in the morning of 24 June 1812. The flanking armies, with

Marie-Louise, Napoleon's Austrian princess bride. (Ann Ronan Picture Library)

another 115,000 men, also began their advance. Less than half Napoleon's men were French.

The Russians were divided into three armies: the 1st, 2nd, and 3rd Armies of the West, deployed over a wide front. The largest of these armies was the 1st, commanded by Barclay de Tolly. His 126,000 men were further subdivided, for the 1st Corps under Wittgenstein was separated by 100 miles from the main army, and Platov's Cossacks were even further away forming a link with Bagration's 2nd Army. Bagration had about 47,000 under his command, divided into two corps. The 3rd Army, under Tormasov, some 45,000 men, was so dispersed that it would take several weeks to bring it together. A further 30,000 reserves under Admiral Chichagov would be called up from the Crimea during the campaign. All told the Russian field armies were outnumbered almost two to one.

Napoleon's strategy was to advance upon Barclay and then turn and crush Bagration when his anticipated advance into Poland brought him into range. Ironically, this fitted well with General Phull's plan for the Tsar. Phull, a Prussian in exile, had convinced the Tsar that a fortified camp at Drissa would act as the anvil to Bagration's hammer. Just prior to Napoleon's invasion, however, others in the Russian high command convinced the Tsar that an initial defensive strategy was required when new intelligence revealed that Napoleon's army was much larger than previously believed. So Bagration's offensive was cancelled. When Barclay fell back toward his camp at Drissa, Bagration began to fall back as well.

The French failure in the 1812 campaign can be attributed to a number of factors. Much of the Franco-Allied army was made up of recent conscripts. These soldiers were not yet accustomed to the rigors of the extended marches that Napoleon required of his troops. Secondly, the supply system broke down. While Napoleon had assembled the greatest logistical train in history, the poor roads and lack of forage prevented the supply wagons from keeping up with the main army. As the supply train failed, discipline went too. Men left the ranks to find food and shelter, and many never returned. The long marches caused the men's health to break down and they died ingloriously from various maladies.

While the terrible hardship of the winter retreat is legendary, the stifling heat alternating with chilling thunderstorms caused more deaths on the march into the interior of Russia than on the exit. Finally, the French were out-scouted throughout the entire campaign. The Russians knew the terrain and the French had few reliable sources of information. Murat, the King of Naples, while dashing and the envy of every allied cavalier as well as the Cossacks, ran his cavalry into the ground. French cavalrymen complained that they seldom had a chance to unsaddle their horses, and the loss of most of the good mounts would undermine many of the later efforts of Napoleon's army and haunt it for the rest of the Napoleonic era.

All these factors combined to doom Napoleon's enterprise. Many losses might have been avoided by a slower advance with frequent stops to rest and allow the supply to catch up. However, that would have eliminated any chance of catching the

Russian army and bringing them to the decisive battle that Napoleon sought. While we are ahead of our story, these causes of the destruction of the Grande Armée were pervasive and had begun to tell from the first day of the invasion. Indeed, the army's exhaustion was already appreciable on the advance to the frontier through Poland.

While his intelligence reports were slow and not very reliable, Napoleon soon came to recognize that his best opportunity for a quick victory was to pin Bagration's army against the Pripet marshes. He devised a pincer movement, hoping to catch the Russians between Davout's 1st Corps, on the left, and Jérôme's army, on the right. Once he arrived in Vilna, recently vacated by the Tsar and the main Russian army command, Napoleon sent Davout and two divisions with cavalry support to move toward Minsk. At the same time, Jérôme was to keep in contact with Bagration's force and trap and destroy Bagration between the two French commands. However, Jérôme had made little progress, and by the time he got his men moving, a violent thunderstorm made the roads virtually impassable. He fell further behind schedule, and compounded his failings by not keeping Napoleon informed of his progress. Jérôme quarreled with his corps commander General Vandamme and then relieved him. This was the only information forwarded to the French emperor. Napoleon's response was to send a blistering letter back, berating Jérôme for letting a wonderful opportunity slip away. He also sent a secret message to Davout, putting him in command should a battle with Bagration appear to be imminent. Jérôme did little to communicate with headquarters and sat in Grodno for a week awaiting orders, despite instructions to press Bagration.

Napoleon commencing the campaign, crossing the River Niemen which was then the Russian frontier. (Musée de l'armee)

Jérôme Napoleon, posing here before one of his palaces, enjoyed a
reputation as a playboy prince. But not content as the King of
Westphalia, he wanted to rival his brother Napoleon as a general.
His failure to perform his role was an important factor in
Napoleon's defeat in Russia. (Roger-Viollet)

For over two weeks Napoleon stayed in Vilna trying to gather the information required to formulate a new plan of attack. He called upon Schwarzenberg to move his army to support Jérôme, leaving only a small corps under Reynier to watch Tormasov's 3rd Army. The latter had been badly underestimated because of poor intelligence. As these orders went out, there was little Napoleon could do but wait. The rain continued and supply suffered.

To the north, Macdonald was slowly advancing on Riga. There was little to oppose him besides the Cossacks, but again the French and Prussian troops proved ineffective in scouting. South of Macdonald, Oudinot was advancing upon the Drina River. Ney was ordered to support him, but in the wooded countryside was unable to keep contact with his fellow marshal.

On 4 July, Napoleon was still in Vilna and Barclay was approaching the fortified camp of Drissa, along with Phull's adjutant, von Clausewitz. He was horrified when they at last arrived upon the scene. The camp was completely inadequate for their purposes and to try to defend it would surely result in a Russian disaster. Barclay's army was being drained of men, like the French, and he needed to rest for several days in order to stop the hemorrhaging.

Alexander was in a nervous state and torn by conflicting advice he was receiving from all sides. Barclay advised retreat upon the line of supply, while Bagration and others would not consider giving up one more foot of Russian soil. Two political camps had developed. One centered on Barclay and various 'foreign' advisors around the Tsar; the other centered on ultra-nationalists who followed Arakcheev and Bagration. These two factions sent advice and poison-pen letters to the Tsar, who vacillated in order to try to keep the peace.

One aspect where the inconclusiveness of Alexander's policies was shown most tellingly was in unity of command. The two main armies under Barclay and Bagration

The *Grande Armée* crossing a river during the advance into Russia. Many of the losses to horses and men occurred during this exhausting march.

1812 Russian campaign to the French invasion of Moscow

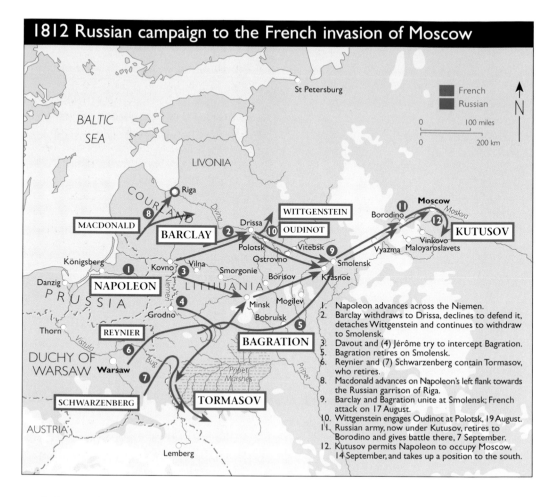

1. Napoleon advances across the Niemen.
2. Barclay withdraws to Drissa, declines to defend it, detaches Wittgenstein and continues to withdraw to Smolensk.
3. Davout and (4) Jérôme try to intercept Bagration.
5. Bagration retires on Smolensk.
6. Reynier and (7) Schwarzenberg contain Tormasov, who retires.
8. Macdonald advances on Napoleon's left flank towards the Russian garrison of Riga.
9. Barclay and Bagration unite at Smolensk; French attack on 17 August.
10. Wittgenstein engages Oudinot at Polotsk, 19 August.
11. Russian army, now under Kutusov, retires to Borodino and gives battle there, 7 September.
12. Kutusov permits Napoleon to occupy Moscow, 14 September, and takes up a position to the south.

needed to act in concert to have any hope of stopping the invader, but no general-in-chief was appointed. Barclay theoretically commanded Bagration by virtue of being minister of war, but Bagration outranked Barclay by seniority and had been Barclay's commander in a previous campaign. It seems that Alexander wanted the coordination to be handled by Barclay, but to avoid the wrath of the ultra-nationalists, he never made this formal. To further complicate the situation, Bagration believed that Barclay was behind a campaign to discredit him and allow the 2nd Army to be crushed. There is no evidence of this, but Bagration was obsessed by the thought.

One thing was certain: as long as Alexander failed to lead, yet remained in the field, Russia's prospects were bleak. A party of generals, led by Arakcheev, and

statesmen, notably the secretary of state Shishkov, convinced the Tsar to leave the front and rally the country to the cause. He left on 19 July and hurried to Moscow, where he called for a raising of more militia.

By 9 July, Napoleon had issued new orders, beginning a concentration between Bagration and Barclay. By now Davout had taken Minsk and was preparing to advance on Borisov. On 12 July Jérôme finally re-established communications with Davout and the two forces were in a good position to attack Bagration. Seeing the opportunity, Davout apprised Jérôme of Napoleon's secret order giving the marshal overall command on this front. Most likely transmitted in Davout's usual blunt manner, the insulted Jérôme quit the army and left the command to Marchand. The latter had no instructions and understandably took several days to sort out the mess. In that time, the opportunity slipped away.

Bagration fought a small battle against Davout's lead column at Saltanovka on 23 July but did not manage to break the French. He retreated and tried to slip around Davout's southern flank.

Barclay's first goal, after Alexander's departure, was to link up with Bagration and interpose himself between Napoleon and Moscow. He headed south-east toward Vitebsk, where he hoped the junction would occur. To protect the route to St Petersburg, he left General Wittgenstein to support General's Essen's men in Riga.

Napoleon had been maneuvering his army to make a strike at Drissa. It took some time before his reconnaissance discovered that the blow would strike air. Finally divining that it was Vitebsk that Barclay was heading for, he turned his army and made for the city. He recalled Oudinot to protect his line of communications. As Oudinot withdrew, Wittgenstein actively harassed him and fought a series of inconclusive actions. This had the effect of pinning Oudinot's men and preventing them from close coordination with the main army. After the first battle of Polotsk, on 18 August, where the outnumbered Russians attacked Oudinot and fought him to a standstill, the front settled down, with both sides digging in.

Barclay barely beat the French to Vitebsk. Marshal Murat had defeated a cavalry rearguard at Ostrovno on 25 July and learned from prisoners that Barclay was ultimately headed for Smolensk. Napoleon's army was in bad shape and exhausted, so Napoleon halted the advance on 29 July and waited for his army to close up and for the lagging supply to arrive. This pause of a week allowed Bagration to swing around Davout's men and head for Smolensk to join Barclay.

Word now reached Napoleon that Tormasov had defeated a portion of Reynier's Corps, a small Saxon force at Kobrin. Napoleon ordered Schwarzenberg back to support Reynier against this unexpected threat. The initiative temporarily passed to the Russians.

Once united with Bagration, Barclay's mind turned to the offensive. He was well aware that the poison tongues of St Petersburg society were railing against the 'foreigner' who had abandoned so much of Mother Russia. If he could now strike successfully, his critics would be silenced, but the continued lack of cooperation from Bagration and then a failure of resolve on Barclay's own part brought the plans to nothing. In the meantime, Napoleon was closing in on the Holy City of Smolensk. Only a heroic stand by General Neverovsky's division at Krasnoi on 14 August prevented the Russian army from being split in two and destroyed.

Smolensk

Neverovsky fell back into Smolensk, a city defended by massive ancient walls, and sent desperate appeals for help. Barclay rushed General Docturov's Corps to the rescue and the French halted to plan for an assault.

The attack began just after noon on 17 August. Leading his men, Marshal Ney drove the Russians out of the surrounding suburbs and several times nearly cut the bridges over the Dnieper River. Napoleon called off the attack at 4.30 pm and brought up more men to continue the next day.

That night, the Russian council of war saw a heated debate between Barclay, Grand Duke Constantine, and Bagration. It was clear that they were getting the worst of the fight, but the Tsar's thick-headed brother and the hot-headed Bagration could think of nothing besides the loss of another provincial capital. Despite the opposition, Barclay ordered the retreat. Smolensk was abandoned. Bagration started his 2nd Army of the West on the road, but in doing so, left a key ford uncovered. After Bagration's withdrawal, Barclay was horrified to find that Ney had crossed many of his men over the river. The Russian counterattack failed to dislodge Ney's men, and much of the 1st Army's supplies had to be abandoned. Barclay started his hurried retreat on the night of 18 August, and his men immediately got lost.

As morning broke on 19 August, Ney's men suddenly came upon Barclay's rearguard about three miles from Smolensk. Probing through the broken terrain, Ney had no idea that he had caught Barclay's main column and was driving in its rear. Barclay turned his men to face the growing threat. The Battle of Valutino swung back and forth for much of the day, as more French troops arrived. At about 4.00 pm Napoleon arrived and ordered Gudin's division of Davout's Corps into the attack. This broke the Russian line. They fell back further to the east and established a new position, and Ney began a bombardment to prepare for yet another assault.

Junot's 8th Corps had arrived on the field to the flank and rear of Barclay's men. Junot had been ordered to cross the Dnieper further downstream and move to support the crossing of the remainder of the army. The moment Napoleon sought had arrived. The fate of the entire campaign might hang in the balance. If Junot sent his men forward, a victory was assured, the only question would have been its magnitude. Murat had moved with Junot and urged him to attack, but Junot said he had no orders. Murat, who himself did not fully appreciate the opportunity, rode off to find better terrain in which to operate his cavalry. Several local attacks were made by Junot's cavalry, on their own initiative, and all were successful. Yet Junot would not budge.

A mile away Ney made his attack as dusk was descending and once more dislodged the Russians. Darkness ended the battle, with the French never knowing how close they had come to winning the war. One more tragic note for the French was that in the final assault, General Gudin was fatally wounded. Gudin was one of the very best French divisional generals, a hero of 1806 and 1809, and from the beginning a stalwart support to Davout.

As the two Russian armies streamed eastwards, their retreat was aided by a five-day rainstorm which allowed them to break contact. Napoleon rested his men prior to resuming the advance on Moscow on 24 August. He had received word that Schwarzenberg had defeated Tormasov at Gorodeczna on 12 August. This had relieved the pressure on the southern flank and left Napoleon in an aggressive mood. His last chance to avoid disaster may have been to halt and spend the winter in Smolensk, but it always appeared that his foe was just within reach. A great victory like Austerlitz or Friedland and the campaign would be his. Three times he had the Russians within reach, only to watch them slip away. While his army was dwindling, were not the Russians also watching their army drain away?

These same questions were haunting the Tsar. With the failure to hold Smolensk, the drum-beat for a 'proper Russian' to lead the army became too much. St Petersburg was militant, demanding a change, and Alexander remembered all too well that his father had been murdered after losing the support of the nobles. He cast about for a general-in-chief and finally, but reluctantly, chose General Mikhail Kutusov. While Kutusov was a hero of the Turkish War and a refined aristocrat, Alexander saw him as an intriguer and moral degenerate, all probably true. Still, the newly created prince had the devout loyalty both of his men and of the xenophobic nobility. Barclay and Bagration kept their positions as commanders of the 1st and 2nd Armies respectively.

Kutusov arrived with the Russian army on 29 August 1812. He held several counsels in which he explained his determination to fight before Moscow while wanting to retreat until he found a proper site to offer battle. It was at Bagration's suggestion that the fields around Borodino were chosen. Kutusov began to deploy his army on the sloping terrain and had redoubts dug on several rises.

Borodino

The leading elements of the French began to arrive on 5 September. They discovered a redoubt near the village of Shevardino,

The battle of Vyazma on the way to Smolensk.
(Roger-Viollet)

which was occupied by Russian artillery and protected by a division of infantry with strong light infantry and cavalry supports. Afternoon was passing, and Napoleon needed to take the position so that he could deploy his men to face the rest of the Russian army waiting for him a mile-and-a-half beyond the redoubt. He ordered in Compans' 5th division of Davout's 1st Corps, supported by two cavalry corps. At the same time the Emperor ordered Poniatowski's Polish Corps to circle to the south and take the position from the flank.

The French came on in skirmish formation and poured a terrific fire into the Russians. The latter responded as best they could, with most damage coming from their cannon. The time had come to take the redoubt, and Compans sent in his best troops. At the point of the bayonet, the Terrible 57th line swept the flanking defenders away and entered the redoubt.

They found not a single man standing left to oppose them. The sun was setting and Prince Bagration mounted an attempt to retake the bloody position. His cavalry had a terrific clash with the French and got the best of it, but could not follow up in the darkness. Bagration claimed to have taken the redoubt and then withdrawn, but their relatively small losses suggest they did little more than skirmishing. What is clear is that the Russians had a stiff fight over a relatively useless position.

Night fell cold and damp, and the French could only look on the Russian campfires with envy as there was little firewood for them to light their own. Napoleon worked through much of the night, making sure that the corps coming up moved to their proper battle positions.

Smolensk 17 August and Valutino 19 August

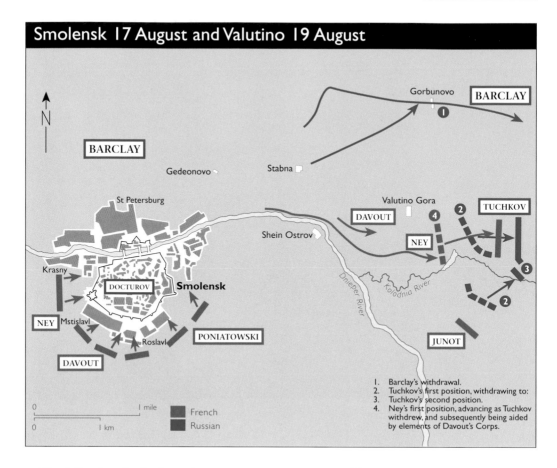

1. Barclay's withdrawal.
2. Tuchkov's first position, withdrawing to:
3. Tuchkov's second position.
4. Ney's first position, advancing as Tuchkov withdrew, and subsequently being aided by elements of Davout's Corps.

French
Russian

The following day both armies reconnoitered their opponent's positions and made plans for the battle. Kutusov had deployed his men on a north-south axis with Barclay's 1st Army in the north, behind the Kolocha River, and Bagration's 2nd Army in the south, anchored in a series of well built redoubts. The lynchpin to Bagration's line, indeed the whole of the Russian position, was the Great Redoubt. This overlooked the crossing point of the river above the village of Borodino. It would have to be taken before Kutusov could be made to yield. Its southern flank was protected by three smaller redoubts called the Fleches, positioned several hundred yards to the left.

Napoleon rode along the front examining the green-clad enemy and watching for any sign that they might once more slip away. He saw none and returned to his tent to rest, for he was feeling ill. There he presented a painting of his son to the Guard. After a while he had the portrait put away, saying that his son was 'too young to see the carnage of the battlefield.' These words were prophetic. An unwelcome omen arrived at about this time. Napoleon received word from Spain of Wellington's defeat of Marshal Marmont at Salamanca.

In his headquarters, Kutusov was spending his time drinking and trading stories with his staff. Most of the final details were left to his chief of staff, Bennigsen. This was not altogether ideal since Bennigsen had no firm idea of what Kutusov had in mind. In several instances he realigned troops to fit his own concepts, not knowing that they disrupted his commander's plans. The most critical among these changes was Bennigsen's moving Tuchkov's Corps out of a hidden reserve position and into an exposed position near the town of Utitsa. This would mean that when Poniatowski's Poles attacked the next day, they fell upon the exposed troops.

During the night, Napoleon had his reserve artillery arrive on the field, adding to the already sizable number of guns. He positioned most of it to begin the battle with a bombardment. At about 6.00 am on 7 September the earth shook as the French line of guns opened fire. The Russians answered with their own cannon and soon the field was covered with a thick blanket of blue-gray smoke. Thousands of solid shot plowed the earth and made bloody messes of those that blocked their path.

Napoleon opened with Eugene's 4th Corps attacking Borodino itself. The French came through the smoke and fell upon the Russian Guard Jaegers. These troops had been battered by the artillery and quickly gave way. The French rashly pursued too far, however, and were themselves defeated. Eugene still held the town and used this position to deploy his guns so as to bring flanking fire upon the Great Redoubt.

Napoleon now ordered his main effort to begin. He wanted to attack the whole of the Russian left flank. To accomplish the assault he sent in three divisions of Davout's

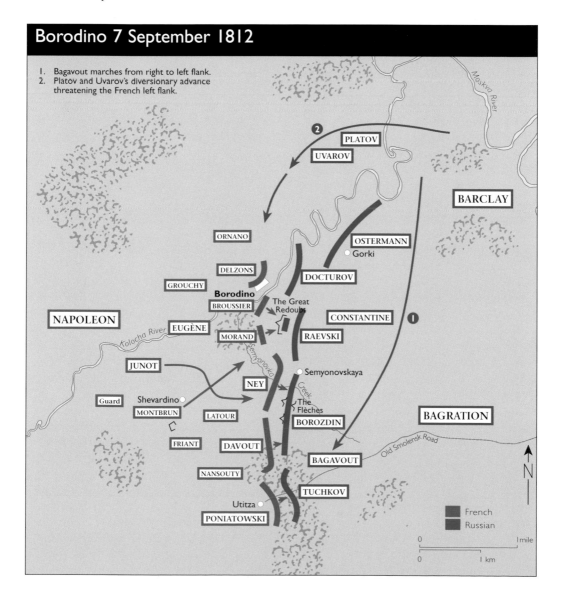

Borodino 7 September 1812

1. Bagavout marches from right to left flank.
2. Platov and Uvarov's diversionary advance threatening the French left flank.

1st Corps against the three Fleches, and he ordered Prince Poniatowski's 5th Corps to attack the position around Utitsa further to the south. In support of both, he had Junot's 8th Westphalian Corps.

Poniatowski had done little fighting in the campaign so far, and was anxious to come to grips with the hated Russians. In his impatience, he drove his men into constricted terrain and had to retrace his steps to meet the enemy. This caused approximately a two-hour delay. Napoleon was unaware of this delay because of the smoke and terrain. The lack of an immediate threat to his front allowed Tuchkov to shift one of his divisions north to aid Borozdin's VIII Corps defending the Fleches. Bagration, whose army was taking these assaults, was riding along his front and feeding in reserves as fast as he could.

Davout's leading division, Compans', drove forward against a terrific pounding delivered by massed Russian guns. Yet his elite 57th was able to seize the first of the redoubts, consolidate, and await the support coming up from Dessaix's division. This support was not forthcoming since Dessaix was intercepted by troops sent by Tuchkov. In a vicious fight along the Utitsa wood-line, Dessaix went down with a critical wound and his men first faltered, then fell back, leaving Compans' men unsupported. Compans went down wounded and Davout took personal command. He too was slightly wounded and his French were ejected by Bagration's grenadier reserves. Seeing the French fall back before him, Bagration sent his supporting cavalry forward in pursuit.

The splendid cavalry dashed down the slope and sabered the running infantry. Their charge carried into the squares formed by Friant's division, held in support by Davout. A swirling melee developed, but was cut short by Murat's French cavalry riding to the rescue. The French cavaliers plowed into the disordered ranks of the Russians and sent them streaming back toward their own lines.

Napoleon now sent forward Ney's 3rd Corps to renew the attack. Moving around Davout's northern flank, he advanced

through the same barrage that had taken such a toll on Davout's first wave. This attack would match the two greatest firebrands in Europe; Ney and Bagration. The red-headed Ney, sword in hand and leading from the front, charged with his men and swept all before them. This time all three Fleches were taken and the supporting guns overrun. Bagration countered by sending in his massed cuirassiers. The pride of the Russian cavalry swept forward and ejected Ney's men from the hard-won positions. Marshal Murat had come forward with his cavalry and was cut off by the unexpected fury of the Russian heavy cavalry charge. Jumping into the middle of a friendly Wurttemberg infantry battalion, he rallied the shaken Germans so that they fended off every attack and were able to withdraw safely.

Kutusov conferring with his generals. Patriotic myth so soon obscured the truth of the 1812 campaign it is hard to tell what Kutusov actually did during the Borodino battle. (Painting by A.V. Kivchenko, Roger-Viollet)

Poniatowski and his Poles were now drawing near to Utitsa. The prospect of coming to grips with the 'defilers' of their homeland gave them all the *élan* needed. Tuchkov had an elite grenadier division waiting for them. The Poles closed to point-blank range and started a firefight. The Russians held on grimly, but when Poniatowski used his superior numbers to overlap the flanks of the grenadiers, Tuchkov ordered his men to set fire to Utitsa and fall back to the woods to their rear. It had been a vicious fight and the Poles now paused to reorganize.

Barclay had been up early and riding the field. He worried about French strength on the left. When the bombardment started, Bagration immediately called for help. Wishing to respond, Barclay ordered Bagavout's II Corps to move to support Bagration. He also shifted more of his army to a central position. The animosity between Bagration and Barclay did not deter the latter from his duty.

It took two hours before Bagavout could get underway and a further hour for him to get into a useful position. This made the delays in Poniatowski's morning attack all the more regrettable: when he was once more able to renew the attack, Bagavout was already arriving on the scene.

The Polish prince had massed his corps' guns and began to pound the hill position behind Utitsa. Tuchkov's artillery was on the point of annihilation when a fresh battery heralded Bagavout's arrival. These guns took up the duel and momentarily stalled the assault. Soon, though, the Poles came on with their infantry and the Russian guns had to retreat. Onward came the two divisions. As they reached the wood-line, they were met by a crushing volley, for not only were the elite grenadiers waiting for them, but many of Bagavout's men had taken up positions. The determined fighting again proved expensive for all involved. Tuchkov took a position at the head of the Pavlov Grenadiers and charged. These troops, perhaps the finest in Russia, swept forward into the Poles. As brave as Poniatowski's men were, the Pavlovs were not to be denied. Soon the entire Polish corps was being pressed back to beyond Utitsa. It was at this point that Tuchkov was struck in the head by a bullet and fell mortally wounded; the Russian counterattack subsequently waned.

Russian officers. (Engraving after Finart, Roger-Viollet)

Napoleon now sent Junot's Westphalians to Poniatowski's support. The North Germans advanced and entered the woods. There they encountered the Jaegers responsible for putting flanking fire into both Poniatowski's and Davout's corps. Pushing them steadily back, Junot's men relieved some of the pressure on the Poles and allowed them to re-form for another effort.

While the combat in the woods was progressing, Ney and Davout had come on again and taken the Fleches once more. Bagration counterattacked and took the positions one last time. As this last attack was sweeping over the redoubts, Bagration was hit in the leg by a shell fragment. He remained on the field to see this last Russian success in his sector and then retired. He died of the wound seven days later.

Ney was in a frenzy and led his men forward once more. Davout did the same and this time the blood-soaked Fleches were taken for good. It was about 11.30 am.

To the north, Prince Eugene had organized his forces to prepare an assault across the river on the Great Redoubt. He first launched a probing attack at mid-morning with Brossier's division. While this made little impact on the Russians, it did provide the intelligence needed to make a more determined assault. This was delivered by Morand's division, who swept up the rise and caught the gunners working the 18 guns by surprise. A fierce hand-to-hand left most of the gunners dead and the French in control of this key position.

General Yermolov, Barclay's chief-of-staff, was leading troops toward the crisis to the south when Morand's attack occurred. Rallying the fleeing troops and calling for all local support, he charged the redoubt. Sensing the crisis, the Russians attacked with a fanatic zeal and overwhelmed the French before further supports could arrive to secure their gain. During this attack General Kutaisov, who commanded Barclay's artillery reserve, heroically led forward an infantry regiment whose flag he grabbed. Killed a moment later, his death meant that the substantial 1st Army artillery was paralyzed for the remainder of the battle.

Eugene now prepared to make an assault three times stronger than before, but a cry went up that a large Russian force was descending on him from the north. This was Platov's Cossacks and Uvarov's line cavalry. Platov, the Ataman of the Don Cossacks, had gone to Kutusov early in the battle and pointed out that nothing opposed him. 'Would it not be a good idea to try and turn the French flank?' Kutusov had approved the plan and Platov had started back to his position to prepare the advance. This decision is the only one that can be definitively attributed to Kutusov during the battle.

The two Russian cavalry formations crossed the Kolocha River and slowly made their way toward Eugene's troops in Borodino. Their attack caused few French losses but cost them a great deal in panic and lost time. It also caused Napoleon to send over some of his reserves to meet the threat. Further, Eugene put off all plans for another attack on the Great Redoubt until he was satisfied that the

The Battle of Borodino, 7 September 1812. Napoleon's illness after the battle meant that there was no pursuit of Kutusov, who withdrew to Moscow. (Engraving by Le Beau, after Naudet, Roger-Viollet)

The last Russian stronghold, besides the
Great Redoubt itself, was the small village of
Semyonovskaya. Ney had earlier made an
attempt to take it, following the final seizure
of the Fleches, but had been repulsed. Next
came Murat's cavalry. The troopers of
Nansouty and Latour-Maubourg were now
committed against the position. Nansouty
attacked south of the town and found the
ground less than ideal for cavalry. His men
ran into firm infantry, and despite their best
efforts could not make them give way. To the

threat had disappeared. 'Uvarov's diversion'
had delayed the French by nearly two hours.

This gave the Russians time to restore
their line and pound the French opposite
them with a merciless bombardment.
The brunt of this fire fell upon the cavalry
assembled for the anticipated attack on the
Great Redoubt. During this barrage General
Montbrun, commander of the 2nd Reserve
Cavalry Corps, was directing his men
when a cannonball tore across his stomach.
He looked down at the gore, said: 'Good
shot,' and fell dead from the saddle.
A similarly terrible fate faced Latour-
Maubourg's 4th Reserve Cavalry Corps,
who stood impotently by and watched
their numbers dwindle.

Kutusov's army held the key position of
the Great Redoubt but was being threatened
by developments occurring to the south. The
final taking of the Fleches threatened
Bagavout as his flanks could now be turned,
but he also faced a new attack by Poniatowski
and Junot. While the tired Russians made the
French pay for the ground dearly, the French
pressure was now irresistible. Finally driven
through the protective woods, Bagavout's
men quickened their retreat and fell a mile to
the rear astride the Old Smolensk Road.

north of Semyonovskaya, Latour-Maubourg's men had fared better. Catching several grenadier regiments out of square, they rode them down and were only stopped when Russian cavalry hit their disordered formations. However, coming fast on their heels was Friant's division from Davout's Corps. Despite a fearful pounding from the Russian guns, Murat urged them on. Friant hurried to the aid of the hard-pressed cavalry and the position was theirs.

Barclay now sent his IV Corps to try to re-take Semyonovskaya. Napoleon had himself come up and he ordered the Guard Horse Artillery to open up on the dense formation of IV Corps. The initial rounds stopped their advance, and the continued fire by the finest artillery in the world had the expected terrible results. In fact, Napoleon now had almost 500 guns pouring fire into the area between Semyonovskaya and the Great Redoubt. Virtually all the remaining troops in good order of Kutusov's army were in this area. Any round fired into this spot could hardly fail to find its mark.

It was now almost 2.00 pm and the French made a massive push to take the Great Redoubt. The three infantry divisions of Broussier, Morand, and Gerard attacked from the front while the cavalry of Montbrun, now under General Caulaincourt, and of Latour-Maubourg hit the flanks. The honor of being the first unit to enter the fort

French and allied cavalry finally storm the Great Redoubt to finish the battle. (Charpentier, Roger-Viollet)

seems to have belonged to the Saxon
Zastrow cuirassiers from Latour-Maubourg's
Corps. This superb unit slaughtered the
gunners as the supporting French quickly
joined in the fight. The resisting Russian
units were destroyed. Caulaincourt chased
off the Russian supporting cavalry opposite
him before swinging in from the rear of the
redoubt to close the trap. Unfortunately, he
would pay for this success with his life.

Grouchy's cavalry, following up the
French attack, now charged into the
remaining Russians. Barclay committed the
Russian Guard cavalry in order to stop them.

The entire Russian line was now shattered.
Barclay re-formed the remaining units on a
ridgeline a mile to the rear. There he waited
for Napoleon's next move. Several marshals
urged their Emperor to send in the Guard and
complete the victory. Napoleon hesitated,
then declined. He reasoned that he was a long
way from home and that his Guard ensured
his survival. It was also not clear to him that
the Russians were entirely beaten. Napoleon,

tired and ill, was satisfied that a victory had
been won. For that day, it was enough.

That night Kutusov sent a message to the
Tsar announcing a great victory. When his
generals asked to retreat he was at first
angered by the suggestion, but as the
evening wore on, it was clear the Kutusov's
army had taken a fearful beating. He had lost
45,000 men out of 120,000. While he did
not know Napoleon's losses (about 30,000),
it became clear that the French were
prepared to fight the next day. The Russians
were low on artillery ammunition as well.
Reluctantly, Kutusov ordered the retreat.

Napoleon had trouble even rising the next
day, 8 September. His illness and the terrible
carnage of the battle had caused a lethargic
depression to set in. It was some time before
he ordered the army to prepare to resume
the advance to Moscow.

When the final reckoning was done it was
clear the Kutusov could not face Napoleon

The fire in Moscow forced even Napoleon to flee.

1812 Russian campaign: The retreat from Moscow

French
Russian

1. Kutusov attacks Napoleon's outposts at Vinkovo, 18 October.
2. Napoleon leaves Moscow, marches south and is blocked at Maloyaroslavets, 24 October.
3. Napoleon retreats; pursued by Kutusov (4), with action at Krasnoe (5), 15 November.
6. Chichagov advances north to intercept Napoleon at the Beresina; Schwarzenberg and Reynier (7) are unable to stop him, and retire subsequently.
8. Napoleon reaches the Beresina on 25 November; Chichagov and Wittgenstein are held off by Victor and Oudinot while Napoleon crosses the river just north of Borisov.
9. Napoleon's retreat continues, reaching Königsberg mid-December; Napoleon himself leaves the army at Smorgonie, 5 December.
10. Macdonald withdraws, and
11. Macdonald's Prussian contingent under Yorck defects at Tauroggen, 30 December.

again until fresh reinforcements had swelled his ranks. So the decision was taken not to defend Moscow. On 14 September the Russian army passed through the city, taking what they could, and marched to the east. The French army entered the capital that same evening. The object of so much hardship was now Napoleon's, but where were the messengers from the Tsar asking for terms?

The French enter Moscow

That same evening Napoleon received an answer of sorts. Fire had broken out in several places in the city. The governor-general of the city, Rostopchin, had ordered that Moscow should burn to the ground rather than be possessed by the French. Ironically, this act of a man driven insane by his responsibility almost saved Napoleon's army. For had much more of the city been incinerated, the Emperor would surely have

started his withdrawal west earlier.

After the first day, the fire seemed to be contained, so Napoleon rode into the city and entered the Kremlin. From here he saw the fire leap up in several new spots and reports came back to him that it was the Russians deliberately setting the fires. Incredulous that men would do that to their own cherished city, he ordered all men caught setting fires shot. He surveyed the situation until it was almost too late. It was only with repeated urgings of his staff that he consented to leave the inferno, barely escaping as the flames closed in around him.

The fire burned for four days and destroyed three-quarters of the city. The French were able to preserve some of the most historic buildings, but the ancient city of the Tsars of Russia was no more. Re-occupying the burnt-out shell, the French sat down and waited for the Russian surrender that they were sure would come.

Napoleon deployed his army in a ring around the city and guarded the approaches from which any attacks might come. The problem was that while the troops immediately around Moscow were still getting regular food, the outlying units were not. This left these men vulnerable to attack as they spread out desperately foraging for something to eat.

Following his retreat from Moscow, Kutusov had taken his army in a wide circle to the south. This left him in a position to receive reinforcements coming up from the Orel region. He also had the option of moving against Napoleon's supply line.

Napoleon sent out several feelers for peace but received no response. Finally he sent General Lauriston on a mission to Kutusov. After meeting with the aged general, Lauriston delighted Napoleon with the news that an emissary had been dispatched to the Tsar. This surely would bring about the desired end to war, so Napoleon decided to put off any thoughts of withdrawal until an answer arrived. This delay proved fatal.

As Napoleon sat in the Kremlin, sending letters to govern his vast holdings, his men had begun to fraternize with the Russians in an informal truce. This laxness led to a surprise attack on Sebastiani's cavalry at Vinkovo. Here were some of the men left to fend for themselves, and they had become scattered when the attack came. It was only the quick thinking of Murat that prevented a major defeat. The dashing King of Naples put himself at the head of the Carabiniers and charged the enemy. The attack sent the Russians reeling back and by the time that they had recovered, the French had restored their order. Seeing this, the Russian attack was abandoned.

The defeat at Vinkovo convinced Napoleon that no peace was in the offing, and he made plans to leave Moscow. Examining the possibilities, the best direction seemed to be a march to the south-west, where he could either take the unravaged route to the west or possibly bring Kutusov to a decisive battle while the French army could still fight. Planning his departure

for several days he slipped out of Moscow on 19 October. This proved to be far too late.

The retreat begins

As Napoleon was pulling out of Moscow, the Russians were going over to the offensive. While Kutusov watched Napoleon's main army, the other armies were to strike the strategic flanks north and south. Admiral Chichagov had joined Tormasov and took command of the combined force. He swung west around the Pripet Marches and moved against Schwarzenberg's rear. When the Austrian gave way and positioned himself to protect Warsaw, Chichagov sent Sacken with 25,000 men to pursue and took his remaining army of 38,000 around to the north of the marshes and headed toward Napoleon's rear. Schwarzenberg reacted by defeating Sacken and heading off in pursuit of Chichagov, but it was clear the Austrian's heart was no longer in the campaign.

To the north, the Russian commander Wittgenstein, who had received large reinforcements, advanced on St Cyr, but divided his command into two parts. Wittgenstein himself was defeated at Polotsk, while his other wing, under Steingell, lost a battle to the Bavarian General Wrede. However, Wittgenstein did succeed in temporarily diverting Marshal Victor's Corps from moving to support Napoleon.

Napoleon planned to make his way back to Smolensk via a southern route. Marching out of Moscow, he headed south for the key town of Maloyaroslavets, which guarded the crossing of the Lutza River. Prince Eugene led with his French troops and upon arrival at the town, on the evening of 23 October, found it free of any enemy. He placed two battalions in Maloyaroslavets, south of the river, and kept the remainder on the better camp site north of the river. What Eugene and Napoleon did not yet know was that their maneuver had been detected by General Docturov and that he had been shadowing the French on a parallel road. Furthermore, he had alerted Kutusov, and

the remainder of the Russian army was in hot pursuit.

Docturov launched an attack on the two isolated battalions before dawn the following day. His men threw back the surprised French and headed for the bridgeheads over the Lutza. Eugene reacted by counterattacking with Delzon's division. They pushed their way into the town but were repelled when they tried to exit on the other side. The Russians were coming onto the field quickly and deployed in a strong position on a ridge above the town. The battle continued throughout the day, with the final outcome much in doubt. Finally, Napoleon, who arrived at the scene, committed sufficient troops to widen the bridgehead so as to allow his army to cross. The battle sputtered to a close with nightfall. The following day, Napoleon rode out to survey the field and consider his prospects. A body of Cossacks swept down and took his small escort by surprise. The outnumbered Guard cavalry was able to repulse the attack, but not before several of the enemy had come very close to the Emperor. Napoleon was visibly shaken by this incident. The

The army of France on its return from Moscow. (Engraving, Roger-Viollet)

prospect of being captured so unnerved him that he ordered his doctor to prepare a pouch of poison that he could take should this ever happen again.

That night Napoleon ordered a council of war to discuss the options with his commanders. This extremely unusual occurrence shows how unsettled he was: he had lost his confidence. Only Murat suggested a renewed attack. The others proposed various courses of retreat. Napoleon ordered the retreat. Ironically, Kutusov had ordered a disengagement as well, for he was sure that his raw army could not withstand another full battle.

The two armies broke away from each other, with Kutusov heading west and Napoleon heading north-west toward Mozhaisk. This line of retreat would take him over the same devastated route that he had taken on the way to Moscow.

Kutusov divided his army, with one wing moving parallel with the French, ready to strike at any opportunity, and the main force

Ney's heroic command of the rearguard made him a legend. (Edimedia)

following a similar course outside of striking distance. He also pushed his cavalry ahead to raid the French outposts and depots.

The French army was strung along 40 miles of road. The troops with intermixed, at least in the beginning, with caravans of carriages bearing loot, camp followers, and French actresses rescued from Moscow. Davout was bringing up the rear, trying to gather all the stragglers and wounded. Kutusov in a earlier correspondence with Napoleon had made it clear that prisoners could expect no mercy from the Russians because of the impassioned feeling against the invaders of Mother Russia. This meant that any French soldier who fell out of line would probably die.

When Napoleon learned that Kutusov was trying to make an end run around his army and destroy the essential depots, he increased the pace and drove his Guard on to Vyazma. This preserved the key depot, but strung out his army even more. The Russians attacked the rear on 31 October and 3 November, but with little effect.

On 4 November, it began to snow. The weather worsened over the next few days and the last semblance of order within the French supply system disintegrated. Every night hundreds of men froze to death. There was little, if any, shelter and men huddled together for warmth. Setting villages on fire became common practice in order to provide some respite from the cold.

As supply broke down, the men began to wander off in search of food. Most would never return, falling victim to the cold or to Cossacks. The French had little left by way of organized cavalry, so any small contingent of men were susceptible to the great bands of Cossack raiders that swooped down on the shivering enemy, slaughtered them, and looted the bodies. In one incident a brigade under General Baraguay d'Hilliers was surrounded and annihilated. Images of Cossack depredations terrorized Napoleon's men.

On the retreat, illness was an almost certain death sentence, and disease became rampant as the men were increasingly malnourished. A healthy well-fed man could have dealt with the cold, but the soldiers of the Grande Armée were starving, sick, and forced marching. A fatalism set in among the ranks and the French high command, as each day they stumbled upon a dead man in the snow who only the day before had been among the 'healthy' ones.

Napoleon halted in Smolensk to try to reorder the army. Discipline had become so bad that the stores of food and clothing were broken into and looted by his men. Vast amounts of supplies were thus wasted. With the army losing cohesion, the Emperor resumed the retreat in an effort to save what he could. His army was now only half the strength it had been in Moscow and dwindling fast. The various corps left Smolensk over the

next four days on the road to Krasnoi.

There Kutusov prepared a trap for the French. As Napoleon and his Guard caught up his army's leading troops on 15 November, the Russians attacked to the French front, flank, and rear, in an effort to split the army in two. The first two attacks failed but the third cut the road.

In the army's vanguard, Napoleon went over to the attack. He sent in his Guard artillery and it more than held its own against the Russians, who were driven from Krasnoi and the battle subsided. That night Napoleon sent his Guard Infantry in a risky night attack against several Russia encampments, reflecting his increased desperation. The bitter cold prevented the enemy from properly deploying pickets, and the Guard exacted a terrible revenge upon the dazed Russians. This French success made Kutusov cautious and he went back to

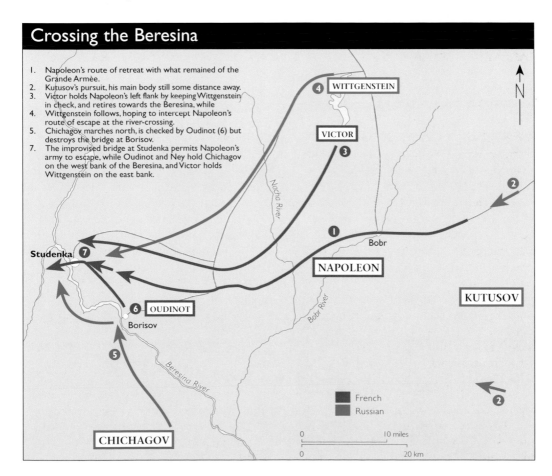

Crossing the Beresina

1. Napoleon's route of retreat with what remained of the Grande Armée.
2. Kutusov's pursuit, his main body still some distance away.
3. Victor holds Napoleon's left flank by keeping Wittgenstein in check, and retires towards the Beresina, while
4. Wittgenstein follows, hoping to intercept Napoleon's route of escape at the river-crossing.
5. Chichagov marches north, is checked by Oudinot (6) but destroys the bridge at Borisov.
7. The improvised bridge at Studenka permits Napoleon's army to escape, while Oudinot and Ney hold Chichagov on the west bank of the Beresina, and Victor holds Wittgenstein on the east bank.

WITTGENSTEIN

VICTOR

NAPOLEON

KUTUSOV

Studenka

OUDINOT
Borisov

CHICHAGOV

Bobr

Nacha River

Bobr River

Beresina River

French
Russian

0   10 miles
0   20 km

striking only when Napoleon was in the process of retreating. The road was open again, at least for a time.

The victory at Krasnoi allowed Napoleon once more to gather his army, with the exception of Ney's Corps. Ney had lingered too long in Smolensk to gather up stragglers and had been cut off. Called on to surrender, he refused and tried to fight his way out. Failing in this, he lit fires to fool the Russians and slipped around the Russian northern flank in the darkness.

The Beresina

When Ney's tiny command rejoined the main army there was rejoicing. The marshal was now lauded by Napoleon as 'the bravest of the brave.' By now Victor had joined Napoleon, swelling the ranks, but Admiral Chichagov had cut off the army at the Beresina River. He had surprised the garrison at Borisov and stood between Napoleon and safety. A thaw had not proved kind, leaving an impassable river. Oudinot, who had taken over St Cyr's command when the latter was wounded, surprised Chichagov's garrison at Borisov and took the depot. The Russians burned the bridge and still had their main force on the western bank of the Beresina. As Napoleon

approached, he was being encircled by three Russian armies: Wittgenstein's, Chichagov's, and Kutusov's. Time was of the essence and it was clear that Schwarzenberg was not going to arrive to attack Chichagov from the rear. A ford had to be found and quickly. By 24 November Napoleon arrived ahead of the main army. Victor was deployed to slow Wittgenstein, Oudinot was demonstrating in front of Chichagov, and the remainder of the army struggled onward towards Borisov.

On the night of 25 November, engineers began building three bridges over the Beresina at Studenka, about 10 miles north of Borisov. Standing in chest-deep freezing water, many of the men sacrificed their lives for these constructions. By late afternoon of the 26 November they were complete and the troops began to cross. Both Oudinot's and Ney's men crossed and took up positions to oppose Chichagov's expected attack. What little remained of the army fought well.

The crossing points were a confused mass of the wounded and stragglers crowding to get over the bridges. Victor's Corps were deployed as a rearguard and for over a day

Many failed to cross the Beresina bridges when they had a chance because they were exhausted mentally and physically. When they realized time had run out, the chaos at the bridges was brutal. (Lithography by V. Adam, Edimedia)

withstood the weight of Wittgenstein's men. By the night of 27 November it was clear that Victor could not hold out much longer. Ammunition was running low and more Russians were arriving by the minute. Just after midnight Victor evacuated the east bank of the river and passed to the other side. There he stood guard over the bridge in order to allow as many stragglers as possible to reach safety. Many were too exhausted and apathetic. Victor preserved the bridge as long as possible, but finally set it on fire, abandoning many to their fate.

The remnant of the French and allied army headed toward Vilna. It was then that the temperature plummeted, and many who had survived that far now died. The Cossacks were about the only troops that could operate off the roads, and daily they added to the French casualties.

Napoleon had received word of an attempted *coup d'etat* in Paris orchestrated by a madman, General Malet. For a day he had taken the reins of power before being arrested, claiming Napoleon had died in Russia. This plot, along with the knowledge that new troops would be needed to continue the campaign, prompted Napoleon to leave the army and return to Paris. On 5 December, he left the army at Smorgonie. While his generals had agreed with the

decision, many in the ranks felt abandoned. Murat was given overall command.

When the army arrived at Vilna, it was a repeat of Smolensk. Stores were sacked and food and supplies wasted. With disorder rampant, Murat ordered the retreat to continue. Ney fought several rearguard actions and kept the Russians at bay. When the army reached the Niemen, it was Ney who on 9 December stayed behind to destroy the last baggage. He then crossed the river and in so doing was the last Frenchman to leave Russian soil, making himself a legend.

One final piece of bad news for the French was that Count von Yorck had defected to the Russians with his men. Yorck, who had led the Prussian half of Macdonald's command, even failed to alert Macdonald of his actions. Macdonald met most of the remaining army in Königsberg where the retreat finally ended on 13 December. The news of Yorck's defection panicked Murat and he left the army, turning over command to Eugene. It was a typical act for the mercurial marshal.

The Grande Armée was dead. Prussia was clearly beginning to rebel and Europe saw Napoleon as vulnerable. The campaign of 1812 was over and the campaign of 1813 was beginning.

Barclay de Tolly and Jacob Walter

Barclay de Tolly: Portrait of a commander

The popular history of the Russian campaign of 1812 comes from Tolstoy's novel *War and Peace*. It is Marshal Kutusov who is portrayed as the great Russian hero of the campaign. This is a great disservice to the real hero, Michael Andreas Barclay de Tolly.

Barclay de Tolly was born on 24 December 1761 in Polish Lithuania. He was descended from a minor Scottish nobleman who had gone to the Baltic to seek his fortune. The Barclays had prospered in the Germanic Lutheran provinces and Michael's father had served in the Russian army prior to receiving his patent of nobility from the Tsar.

Michael grew up in St Petersburg where he was raised by his aunt. This was a common occurrence among the German Protestants and gave the young man the exposure to upper society unavailable in the Baltic provinces. His foster-father was also in the military and enrolled the young Barclay in a cavalry regiment at the age of six. He would spend the rest of his life within the military.

Barclay's schooling was basic, but he was a voracious reader and pursued studies beyond the normal requirements. Among his acquired talents was a fluency in Russian and French, to accompany his native German. He also devoured anything that would expand his military knowledge.

During his youth he developed a quiet, taciturn personality quite in keeping with his German upbringing. His contemporaries described him as meticulous, brave, honest, modest, bright, and somewhat humorless.

Barclay joined the Jaegers in 1787 and his unit joined the army of Prince Potemkin (of Potemkin Village fame). Here the captain caught the attention of his superiors and became an aide to one of the wing commanders, Prince Anhalt-Bernburg. During the victorious siege of Ochakov against the Turks, Barclay participated in the desperate sortie in which most of his fellow officers were casualties, including the severely wounded Mikhail Kutusov.

Barclay continued to serve with distinction until 1789, when he was transferred to the Finnish front. The ongoing hostility between Russia and Sweden turned to war when King Gustavus decided to take advantage of Tsarina Catherine's Turkish war to move troops into his Finland province with an eye toward taking St Petersburg. The addled king lacked good organization, however, and when Russia's ally, Denmark, invaded Sweden in support of Russia, Gustavus' attention was diverted, giving Catherine time to move enough troops into place to counter the Swedish threat. The war was bloody and inconclusive on both sides and came to a halt when Sweden's internal problems caused the king to end the war with things back to pre-war status.

For Barclay, marriage to his cousin followed the next year before a posting as major and battalion commander of the St Petersburg Grenadier Regiment sent him to Poland to participate in its partition. The war lasted till 1793 and flared up again the following year when the Poles under Kosciuszko revolted. Distinguishing himself at the battles of Vilna and Grodno, he continued the campaign under General Suvorov when the Warsaw suburb of Praga was stormed. This brutal event ended the rebellion and led to the final destruction of what remained of Poland. Barclay was promoted to lieutenant-colonel for his conduct and to full Colonel in 1796. He remained in Russia commanding the 3rd Jaegers, missing Suvorov's campaign in

Barclay de Tolly, to whom the lion's share of the credit should go for a reformed and reinforced Russian army for the 1812 campaign. (Roger-Viollet)

Italy and Switzerland but performing with such efficiency that he was promoted to major-general in March 1799.

When war against Napoleon came in 1805, Barclay was posted under Bennigsen. Fortunately Bennigsen's army avoided the debacle of Austerlitz, though its arrival there may have swung the balance. There was to be no promotion for battlefield heroics, but neither was there any blame.

The war came to life again for the Russians in 1806 as they moved to support their Prussian allies. Unfortunately, they were unable to arrive before Napoleon crushed the Prussians at Jena-Auerstadt and

the pursuit that followed. The leading Russians took up their positions around Warsaw and awaited the French and their supporting armies. Napoleon moved upon them quickly and after forcing a river crossing fought the twin battles of Pultusk and Golymin. It was at the battle of Pultusk that Barclay, by now a lieutenant-general, received his baptism of fire as a commanding general. Leading one of the advance guards, his men faced the brunt of the redoubtable

Barclay's great rival, Prince Bagration. Despite his great suspicions of his fellow general, Bagration did finally join Barclay at Smolensk. He became a Russian martyr for his mortal wound at Borodino. (Roger-Viollet)

Marshal Lannes' attack. A desperate fight in the woods swung back and forth. Lannes, realizing the French were facing the main Russian army and not a rearguard, broke off the attack. Barclay won praise for his calm, skillful performance

The three advance guards were consolidated under the command of Prince Bagration. Barclay led the most active troops of this command. He continued the campaign and covered himself with glory for several rearguard actions. At Eylau on 7 February 1807, his men defended the village against determined assaults by the

French. It was only an attack of the Old Guard that finally expelled Barclay's men. Once more he mounted a counterattack. Barclay, leading cavalry, was hit by canister in the arm and narrowly avoided being crushed by the stampede of horses before one of his men scooped him up.

After being rushed to a hospital in Konigsberg, Barclay's arm was saved. However, this wound would never fully heal, nor would Barclay ever again have the full use of the arm. It was serious enough that he would not be fit for action again until after Friedland and the Russian surrender at Tilsit. During his convalescence Barclay became friends with the Tsar. Visiting his wounded general in the hospital, Alexander was struck by Barclay's modest and honest character – a welcome contrast to the vain, preening degenerates who so often surrounded the young Tsar.

Following the Peace of Tilsit, Napoleon suggested to his new Russian allies an attack on Sweden. This served the French needs in two ways: first it would close one of Britain's most lucrative ports left in Europe; and secondly it would draw Russia away from central European affairs. Still, an attack on this traditional enemy was very appealing to Tsar Alexander. The campaign got underway, with Barclay commanding a column in the main army. After initial successes the tide turned against the Russians as all of Finland rose up in a guerrilla war. Barclay showed initiative to the point where he disobeyed a direct command in order to save a contingent which was about to be crushed. Demands were made in the army hierarchy to have him court martialed, but defenders arose to support Barclay. In the end the Tsar sided with Barclay and he was promoted to Governor of Finland.

The second phase of the war called for a crossing of the frozen Gulf of Bothnia. This scheme seemed insane since it called for crossing the frozen waters– a march of 24 miles, a brief rest on a snowy islet, then another 36 miles over the ice. Throughout they would be subjected to the near-arctic winter with no possible protection. Despite these tremendous obstacles, Barclay led his men safely to the Swedish side of the gulf and captured the fortified city of Umea. This legendary effort was temporarily lost in the news that a coup d'etat had overthrown the King of Sweden and peace had been declared.

Barclay remained as Governor of Finland until the end of 1809. His careful and efficient performance earned him Alexander's praise and promotion to Minister of War on 20 January 1810. He immediately set about reforming the field regulations. This massive effort was compiled and distributed in what became known as the 'Yellow Book' because of the color of its cover. This was the first change to be made to the regulations since the days of Peter the Great in the early 1700s.

He next lobbied to establish a series of defensive fortifications along the frontier. While he started the program, little was completed prior to the 1812 campaign. It was his belief that the Russians should be passive in the campaign and grudgingly fall back upon their lines of communication until they could effectively counterattack. This is not to say that he advocated a total Fabian strategy, rather that he believed that trading space for advantage was a sound option. This policy set him at odds with Bagration, who felt that any abandonment of Russian soil was a sin.

When the war began, he was directly under the command of the capricious Tsar and dutifully fell back on the camp of Drissa. It was only after the Tsar's departure that he was able to formulate his own plan. He fell back toward Smolensk and prepared to take the initiative. Bagration joined him with his army and graciously placed himself under Barclay's command.

It was only now that Barclay seemed to lose his nerve. He vacillated between attack and a further retreat. He sent confusing orders and had his troops marching in circles. When Napoleon made a move on Smolensk he regained focus and orders became firm and clear. Following the battle, Barclay decided on a further retreat, and the generals around him became enraged.

He had been under suspicion for being a 'foreigner' and his behavior brought this criticism to a new height. Tsar Alexander felt a change was required and placed Mikhail Kutusov in overall command. Barclay took this demotion with equanimity and performed heroically at the following battle of Borodino. At that battle, Bagration was mortally wounded. With his great rival gone, Barclay continued to act as the 1st Army commander. A fortnight after the fall of Moscow the two armies were consolidated. Soon thereafter Barclay left the army and Kutusov for reasons of health, but in reality, with the joining of the two armies, his role was at an end.

He took no further part in the 1812 campaign, but was placed in charge of the Russian 3rd Army in February 1813. He maneuvered skillfully and once more earned the confidence of the Tsar. Following the twin defeats of Lutzen and Bautzen, Barclay was made commander-in-chief of all Russian armies. He remained in the field at the Tsar's side throughout 1813 and entered France for the campaign of 1814. He was promoted to field marshal for his service.

In 1815, Barclay organized the army for a second invasion of France following Napoleon's return. Though he saw no fighting, he was made a prince of Russia. He continued his role as commander-in-chief for the next three years, when ill health caused him to ask for a leave of absence. The Tsar, wishing to reward this most loyal servant, granted him a two-year leave and 100,000 rubles for expenses.

Barclay was not to enjoy this rest, for on his way to a spa in Bohemia he stopped at one of his homes near Riga for a rest. He died that night, 25 May 1818, apparently of a heart attack.

In the end it was his organizational skills, more than his bravery, that had proved the more valuable to Russia. By preserving the Russian army, he set the stage for Napoleon to make the fatal error of advancing too far and remaining too long in Russia. His steadying influence may have made the crucial difference in Russia's struggle.

Jacob Walter:
Portrait of a common soldier

Jacob Walter, from Wurttemberg (now in south-west Germany) was drafted into the army in the autumn of 1806. He was inducted into the 4th (or Franquemont) Infantry Regiment and sent to guard Napoleon's line of supply as the campaign moved into old Poland. During 1809 he fought the rebels in the Vorarlberg who were attacking Napoleon's rear. During the campaign of 1812 his regiment was part of Ney's Corps. Apart from fighting at the battle of Smolensk, he participated in no major action. He followed the army during the retreat and was mustered out of the regiment for reasons of poor health upon returning home in 1813.

There was nothing remarkable about him and he contributed little to the war effort, but he was an honest chronicler of his experiences and he recorded the attitudes common among the German soldiers of his day.

Walter had been brought up a Catholic, the brother of a priest. This had allowed him the opportunity to learn to read and write. While he considered himself devout, he exhibited relative or situational morals. Stealing was wrong, unless you needed something. Kindness to your fellow men was to be shown at all times, unless they were peasants in an enemy land. It is interesting that Walter sowed his wild oats in 1806, 'an element of my youth', but became religious during the retreat from Moscow.

In 1807, Walter was guarding a rear area when a spy was brought in. The evidence seemed clear enough, so the man was whipped 150 times prior to being shot. There seemed to be no purpose for the flogging other than the amusement of the soldiers and officers, but Walter found nothing odd in this. Following this incident, he was sent out to requisition food from the local villages. Not having a map, he sought a local guide. Naturally, he picked on the most down-trodden section of society to find his man, the Jews. The man tried to hide but

was found and dragged down two flights of stairs. His misery was of great amusement. Walter's attitude was typical of the time, and he never noted any disapproval among his comrades.

The process of finding food often differed little from outright theft. The peasants in their huts made of straw could not defend themselves against pillaging troops. On one occasion, Walter shot a pet dog for his own amusement and then was surprised that the locals were uncooperative.

Walter had contempt for other beliefs, including the Prussian Lutheranism. He observed that these people were superstitious, while exhibiting his own superstitions on repeated occasions. The ideas of the Enlightenment had not penetrated far beyond the upper and educated classes.

Walter's fondest recollections were of his family. The highlight of a campaign was when his regiment was stationed in the same place as his brother's.

In 1809 Walter's battalion was sent to put down the rebellion in the Vorarlberg, which had risen in sympathy with the Tyrol. He saw action in the fighting around Bregenz on 29 May, where he gained experience as a skirmisher. Taking a position on the staircase of a building, he shot off most of his ammunition before making a mad dash to the rear. In the subsequent fighting in the town, he shot a man at point blank range. At no other time does he mention that he actually hit an opponent. At Bregenz, where his men made a hurried withdrawal, Walter makes it quite clear that he considered his running ability his key asset.

Complaints about the local breads and grain, which differed from those at home, were typical among soldiers at the time and Walter makes repeated comments throughout his memoirs.

In 1812 his regiment marched to the Russian border. Throughout the march, he was unaware of the ultimate destination. This was the only time he remembered seeing the high command. The Crown Prince ordered his Wurttembergers to go through maneuvers when it was a holiday.

This was pointed out by one of the lesser ranking Wurttemberg generals and the prince threatened to arrest him. It seems that the prince was annoyed that he had had his command placed under Ney, and was taking out his displeasure on his men.

Walter remembered the march into Russia for its heat, choking dust, and long downpours. He soon began a campaign-long effort to find food. Often the only food available had to be purchased from the despised Jews. The irony that his salvation lay in their willingness to sell to him was lost on him.

At Smolensk, Jacob Walter fought in the only major battle of his military career. His blue-coated comrades and he assaulted the bridgeheads in an effort to cut off the city's defenders. Breaking into the city, he saw the devastation of the fires caused by the battle. His impression was one of total chaos. Finally he rested near a hospital station, to be treated to the sight of piles of amputated limbs.

Walter did march past the carnage of the battle of Borodino, but made little comment about it. By the time he reached Moscow, his company was down to 25 men, from a starting strength of about 175.

During the retreat, Walter became the servant or batman of a major. This he hoped would provide him with a better chance of survival, but it soon was clear that the major depended more on Walter than vice-versa. Hunger was a daily concern and the resulting weakness led to disease and death all along the march. Lice covered every part of his body and the cold wore him down. If he had not stolen a horse, he thought he would have perished; instead someone else did. Indeed, Walter claimed that no-one survived without a horse. This was an exaggeration,

but clearly it was important, since the soldiers kept stealing each others' horses.

Near Borisov he was reunited with a fellow Wurttemberger, cold and wet from fording a river, who shared his loaf of bread with Walter. For this Walter pledged a lifetime's devotion. They finished their meal and mounted their horses to continue the journey, but the generous friend was dead by morning.

The horror of the Beresina crossing is told, with dazed men sitting down in the snow, never to rise. It was here that Walter saw Napoleon. He comments on the unmoved expression on the Emperor's face, though it is hard to believe that he got close enough to get a good look. It is more likely that he projected his own disillusionment.

Near Vilna, he was with a small group of men when the Cossacks came upon them. At first he tried to flee, but he was stabbed at and knocked off his horse. He lay in the snow and did not move while his compatriots were massacred. Finally the Cossacks rode off and Walter stole away to rejoin the army.

At the Niemen he met up with some Westphalian soldiers. Offered hospitality by some local peasants, the men were plied with alcohol and soon set upon and murdered. Walter escaped only by sensing a trap at the last moment.

On Christmas eve, he finally reach a place where he could bath and get a change of clothes. The filth and lice were caked on like 'fir-bark.' Soon he had his first square meal in months and headed back home with a supply and hospital train. On reaching Wurttemberg his was mustered out of the army for reasons of ill health. He returned home and made a full recovery within a couple weeks.

Vienna

Vienna was a changing city in 1809. The austere moralism of Emperor Leopold had been replaced with easier virtue and good times. The cafes were teeming with people and there was much more freedom of thought than a generation earlier. One craze that swept Vienna was the waltz. This dance originated at the turn of the century, developed from an Austrian creation, the *Ländler*. At first the quick whirling around the floor of partners locked in an embrace was thought scandalous, but by 1809 polite society had long since given up their objections and joined the dance floor.

In some ways, though, Vienna was still the product of her great empress, Maria Theresa. The Imperial edifices that adorned the capital were by and large her handiwork. True, the walls that had withstood the two sieges by the Turks, in 1529 and 1683, still encircled the main city, but what lay within exemplified the majesty of the Habsburg dynasty. Vienna was filled with magnificent churches and palaces. Of equal importance to the Viennese were the theaters and opera houses which nightly were filled with the music of the greatest collection of composers ever assembled. Mozart, Gluck, Haydn, and Beethoven have left a legacy unsurpassed to this day.

Franz Joseph Haydn (1732–1809) was the dominant composer in the years leading up to 1809. He is most famous for developing the classical style. This new style was considered liberating when compared to the older Baroque style. Music was mostly written for wealthy patrons, usually ecclesiastic or aristocratic. In Haydn's case it was the Esterhazy family, for whom he worked from 1761 till his death.

Haydn acted as a bridge in the classical music period. He was a contemporary of Wolfgang A. Mozart (1756–1791), and went on to be an instructor of Ludwig von Beethoven (1770–1827). He was popular throughout his career and died wealthy. He was one of the few non-Italian or non-French composers that Napoleon greatly admired. This sentiment was not returned by Haydn, however, perhaps wisely for his career in Vienna.

As the French approached Vienna in 1809, Haydn was already dying. Napoleon had a guard put on his home out of admiration for the great composer. Haydn died on 31 May 1809 and his funeral was held at the Schottenkirche, where Mozart's *Requiem* was performed. His casket was surrounded by French soldiers acting as a guard of honor. His body was transported through the lines, where an Austrian honor guard took over from their French counterparts. He was buried at Hundsturm Churchyard near his home.

Even 18 years after his death, the shadow of Mozart still cast his mark upon Vienna. He had been typical of the composers of the period, working for patrons, but had alienated them in one way or another. Specifically, his flirting with themes that cast the nobility of the time in a less than favorable light and had left him without patronage. Friends supported him and gave him commissions to write for the *Opera Buffa*. Mozart took to comic opera and wrote such enduring works as *The Marriage of Figaro* and *The Magic Flute*. Twenty years later all society now flocked to the theaters to see this style, and Mozart was much more popular than he had been during his lifetime.

The classical music era was at its height in 1809, and part of the change was the instrumentation of the works being composed. The piano had replaced the harpsichord, and the mark of the new style was a composer's production of music for the piano. The ability to vary the level of sound produced a dynamism that seemed in keeping with the spirit of the new thinking pervasive after the French Revolution.

Personifying this thinking was Beethoven. He was imbued with the ideas of Republicanism, and had renounced his admiration of Napoleon upon hearing of him taking the crown of France. His vibrant works were popular among all classes and he was evolving the medium to a point that a new age called Romanticism would follow, with many of his works being in the vanguard. It is amusing to reflect that his most popular works of that time were rather pedestrian, such as *Wellington's Victory*, a piece celebrating the British victory at Salamanca in 1812.

The Viennese people were perhaps the most cosmopolitan in the world at the time. While they would nearly bankrupt themselves in trying to defeat the French, they made a distinction when it came to Napoleon. He was, after all, the most famous man alive. Dezydery Chlapowski, an aide to Napoleon, describes the reaction Napoleon received when he first arrived at the gates of the city:

'Here I saw a sight which I would not have believed had I not seen it with my own eyes and heard it with my own ears. The city walls were not crowded, but there were still a good many well-to-do inhabitants on the ramparts. The Emperor rode right up the glacis, so only a ditch 10 meters wide separated him from these people. When they recognized him, they took off their hats and began cheering. I could only explain such behavior by the devotion which a man like the Emperor inspired in all around him.'

It is little wonder that the French soldiers found Vienna a pleasurable place to spend time.

Louise Fusil

Napoleon's army had found a flourishing French colony in Moscow. Some of these émigrés had fled the political persecutions of the French Revolution, but many others were artists and tradespeople seeking to tap the Moscow market. Among the Russian aristocracy, fashion and the arts still imitated French styles, so there had been plenty of opportunities for ambitious French people. While Fedor Rostopchin, the governor of Moscow, had taken the director of the French theater company as a hostage, the rest of the troupe had been left behind. The French decided to celebrate their victory by enjoying some good plays.

The performers had suffered growing hostility from the suspicious Moscow populace. Now they had the honor of performing for Napoleon himself and his glittering entourage. Some officers sniffed that the performance was not up to Paris standards, but the actors must have thought their luck had changed. The 38-year-old actress Louise Fusil enjoyed not only a new protector, an urbane soldier-diplomat, General Armand de Caulaincourt, but also the distinction of being asked by Napoleon himself for an encore of a song.

Distracted by the company of the most powerful men in the world, it came as a complete surprise to Louise when a French officer told her the army had to leave Moscow. Fearing what the Russian soldiers would do when they saw the wreckage of Moscow, Louise decided it would be wise for her to leave. She hoped she could find sanctuary in Minsk or Vilna until calm was restored and she could safely return to Moscow. Many other actresses and French and allied civilians also decided that safety lay in following the French army. She thought herself fortunate to be offered a ride in the splendid carriage of Caulaincourt's

nephew, also on Napoleon's staff. Though the weather struck her as beautiful, fortunately she remembered to bring her furs.

The carriage was designed to allow its occupant to sleep in comfort, so Louise was comfortable during the first stage of the retreat. The pace was punishing, and outside the wounded were being abandoned, food distribution had ceased, and the nights were getting very cold. The horses began failing, and some were not even dead before the starving troops clamored to cut them up before the flesh froze. At this stage women and children were still getting help, but the bonds of comradeship were fraying fast.

Louise, close to headquarters, was spared much of this. Nothing would have been funnier at other times, she thought, than the sight of an old grenadier, with his mustache and bearskin, covered in pink satin fur. But the poor fellow was perishing from cold. She narrowly evaded disaster when the coachman carelessly let two of the horses freeze to death one night. The two remaining could not pull the carriage and she desperately considered ways to continue, but the driver managed to turn up with two replacements, obviously stolen.

Another general took pity on her and detached a gendarme to see her through the chaos that surrounded the column. Outside Smolensk, a Guard colonel held up her carriage, accusing it of blocking his regiment, threatening to have it cast aside despite the servant's insistence of the august rank of its owner. The sight of Louise softened his heart: 'Oh, I'm sorry, I didn't realize there was a lady inside,' he said.

Louise had to smile at him, for the grenadier colonel was covered in blue satin fur. He had not lost his sense of humor yet, and soon turned into another protector. He shared his dinner with her in his quarters,

The sight of Napoleon, like this, without his famous hat and showing the strains of campaigning demoralized one of Louise's fellow actresses. (V. Vereschagin, Roger-Viollet)

but in the cold there was nothing romantic about it. In the end she had to abandon her carriage to get through the crush at the gates of Smolensk. Yet to her surprise, the carriage turned up again though it had been looted, by Cossacks it is said, though probably by the servants. What food was available in Smolensk was selling at famine prices and even the servants of prominent courtiers were in danger of starving.

In Smolensk, Louise regained the company of her fellow actresses. One of them was rattled. Napoleon himself had come over to give her some words of comfort, but his headgear, a green velvet bonnet trimmed with fur, instead of his trademark hat, struck her as incongruous and sinister.

Still, the actresses were able to get out of Smolensk as far as Krasnoi. There the Russians had cut the road: Louise saw cannonballs bouncing across it. The carriage was abandoned again, and the horses were used to carry the actresses cross-country. However, the horses were exhausted and the snow very deep, and soon they were able to go no further. Louise struggled into town on foot. Remarkably the Polish coachman, who Louise regarded as a careless brute, was resourceful enough to go back later and recover the carriage.

Krasnoi was a nightmare. Alone amongst the mob, Louise found no-one who could direct her to Imperial Headquarters. An officer told her it had already gone. Knowing she was not able to catch up with it, her strength failing, Louise resigned herself to die. She found herself falling asleep. Death by cold seemed very gentle, and the shaking given to her by a savior seemed very annoying. She passed out, and woke to find herself in a room surrounded by officers. One of the Emperor's surgeons had saved her life by wrapping her in furs and placing her in a quiet corner. Placing a frozen person next to a big fire, as some officers had tried to do with her, could have been fatal.

Marshal Lefebvre, the grizzled war-horse, regarded her with interest. He was one of those who had picked her up out of the snow in the street. As she thawed out, he brought her some coffee. Louise had found a new protector. Soon she was in the marshal's carriage, following behind a Guard detachment. Behind, the road was littered with abandoned wagons and artillery and many corpses. Ney and his corps were far behind, presumed lost. One of her actress friends made it out of the debacle perched atop one of the few remaining cannons.

On to Liady, where the dignitaries of the Imperial Headquarters packed into some of the squalid houses of the poor Jewish inhabitants. A few miserable potatoes were extorted from the Jews with threats or gold. Louise was more considerate than most: 'They were Jews, but at least living beings. I'd gladly have embraced them.' Outside the crowded shelter, the unlucky ones were dying by the battalion.

On to the Beresina. The old warrior Marshal Lefebvre had grown a white beard, and leant on a knobby stick. At the bridges, Napoleon himself stood, seeming to Louise to be as calm as he would be at a Paris review. 'Don't be frightened, go on, go on,' Napoleon said, presumably to her as she was the only woman present.

Characteristically, Murat did not miss a chance to flirt with a pretty woman. He stood at her carriage door, chatting, dressed like a hero in a melodrama she thought, even to the undone collar in the biting cold. The favored Louise experienced a different Beresina than most, but even she thought she heard from a mile or so away the scream of the many stragglers lost on the far bank when the bridges were broken and the Russian artillery opened on them. Marshal Lefebvre was as tough as a soldier could be, but she saw even he turned pale at the ghastly sound.

Some of her fellow actresses did not make it across the Beresina. Some were rounded up by the Cossacks and spared perhaps, as were many of the officers. The rank and file were given no quarter. At Vilna was another bottleneck where more of the French civilians from Moscow died, unable to get through the crowded gate to the shelter within. Louise did get through thanks to Lefebvre and Murat, and there she repaid one of her benefactors, volunteering to stay behind to nurse and protect Lefebvre's sick son. Besides, she was sick, exhausted too, and the French army, abandoned by Napoleon, had still a long way to go to safety, beset by Cossacks all the way.

Twenty thousand French were left behind in Vilna to fall into Russian hands, three to four thousand of them officers, some of them the poor civilians who mistakenly left Moscow in the army's protection. Even after the Russians arrived, many were to die of privations and an epidemic of typhus. Louise survived to write her memoirs. If it was like that for a pampered actress, what must have it been like for the less fortunate?

Napoleon under pressure

The destruction of the *Grande Armée* in Russia was the greatest disaster, both militarily and politically, to have befallen Napoleon since he came to power. With his enemies determined to continue the fight, Napoleon had to find a way of opposing them. That he did so is testimony both to his own determination and to the resources of his empire.

Although the retreat from Moscow had ended at Konigsberg, this was not a position that could be held. Before leaving the army, and before turning over commmand to Eugene, Murat had placed most of his serviceable troops into Danzig, where a considerable force was to remain besieged until they were compelled to surrender on 29 November 1813. These troops were thus denied to Napoleon for operations in the field; but having called off the pursuit of the remnant of the *Grande Armée*, the Russians waited until the spring of 1813 before recommencing major offensive movements. This gave Napoleon a respite of a few months in which to assemble a new army to support the troops already in Germany, a force insufficient on its own to resist a determined Russian advance.

Napoleon's problems were not even concentrated in this one area of operations. Since 1807 increasing numbers of French troops had been engaged in the Pensinsular War, which had arisen from Napoleon's attempt to occupy the Iberian peninsula by deposing the Spanish monarch and replacing it with his brother Joseph, who had been proclaimed as king of Spain in June 1808. This was so unpopular that most of Spain rose in revolt which, aided by the presence of the energetic and successful British army commanded by Arthur Wellesley (later Duke of Wellington), had turned the French occupation into a

running sore, a 'Spanish ulcer' as Napoleon described it, which constituted a severe and continual drain upon his resources. By the end of 1812, the war in Spain had turned decisively against the French; by the end of the following year they would be expelled from the Peninsula, and southern France would be threatened with invasion (see Osprey Essential Histories, *The Napoleonic Wars: The Peninsular War 1807-1814*, by Gregory Fremont-Barnes). Napoleon's decision to withdraw numbers of experienced troops from Spain, to assist him in continuing the fight in Germany, served only to make the French position in Spain even worse, and confirmed the fatal difficulty of attempting to maintain campaigns upon two widely separated fronts.

For the remainder of his new army, Napoleon drew some troops from internal security units and recalled retired veterans, but assembled most from newly or recently conscripted men. In the following months, such was the demand for troops that conscripts were called up years before they were due officially, resulting in regiments filled with increasing numbers of ever-younger recruits; experienced officers and NCOs trained them, but they did not possess either the experience or the physical abilities of the battle hardened men lost in Russia. Nevertheless, in numerical terms Napoleon was able to field an impressive army for a campaign which was to begin in spring 1813, even if it was deficient in cavalry, the most difficult troops to replace.

Napoleon's defeat in Russia also had the most profound political consequences, beginning with the Convention of Tauroggen (30 December 1812) by which General Hans David von Yorck's Prussian contingent of the *Grande Armée* signed a pact of neutrality with the Russians. This was done without reference to King Frederick William III of Prussia, nominally Napoleon's ally, and together with elements within the Prussian military and civil establishments which were strongly anti-French, it placed great pressure upon the king to take a stronger stance against Napoleon. The situation was compounded when Austria also adopted a position of neutrality, and Schwarzenberg's troops, which had formed the right flank of the advance of the *Grande Armée* against Russia, retired to Austrian territory, compelling the remaining French and allied forces in Poland to retire further west. These measures caused great concern among Napoleon's German allies of the Confederation of the Rhine, many of whose troops had been lost in Russia, but despite their misgivings, these states remained loyal to Napoleon at least for the earlier stages of the 1813 campaign. This was not the case with Prussia: emboldened by the

catastrophe that had overtaken Napoleon in 1812, on 28 February 1813 that state secretly joined Russian by the Treaty of Kalisch, and as French forces withdrew westwards to regroup, Prussia declared war on Napoleon (16 March 1813).

Napoleon still enjoyed some advantages as the campaign of 1813 opened, notably 'unity of command' in that all his resources were under his control, whereas his enemies were to some degree mutually distrustful and lacked co-ordination. Thus upon the renewal of hostilities, Napoleon was to enjoy some successes, but the entry of Austria into the war against him (12 August 1813) was to cause a fatal shift in the balance of power. Supported by a tide of public enthusiasm, the 'War of Liberation' in Germany was to cause the collapse of the Confederation of the Rhine as Napoleon's allies changed sides, and France itself was to be laid open to invasion; all consequences of Napoleon's catastrophic decision to invade Russia in 1812.

Conclusion and consequences

The campaign which had set out to bring Alexander to his senses and close off Russian ports to Great Britain had ended in disaster. Britain, which had been hard-pressed financially in 1810/11, was resurgent. Only the war with the United States prevented her from pouring massive subsidies into the Continent.

Napoleon had started the campaign with 600,000 men and when it had finished, 400,000 had died or never returned to the ranks. The massive loss of horses further compounded the tragedy, crippling the French army in its future campaigns, as they were unable to exploit their victories or transport supplies, artillery, and the wounded.

Russia had lost some 250,000 men and was almost as battered as France, but Alexander, now in the grips of a growing messianic complex in which he saw himself as God's deliverer and Napoleon as the Antichrist, determined to pursue the war, against the wishes of Kutusov.

One key to the future was the defection of the Prussian General Yorck, who made a private treaty with the Russians and his entire contingent changed sides. This event precipitated Prussia's entry into the war against Napoleon. At the same time, Austria withdrew from Napoleon's coalition and waited on the sidelines for further developments.

Napoleon hurried back to France to rebuild his army. He did a remarkable job but his German allies were increasingly war-weary and questioning of the benefits of remaining within the French sphere. Sweden, directed by Bernadotte, was

Eventually the exhausting pace and killing cold reduced most of the *Grande Armée* to every man for himself. (Roger-Viollet)

preparing to join in the alliance against France. The story in Spain was no better: things had definitely turned against the French, and Napoleon needed to take troops out rather than send in more.

Europe was now transfixed by the clear vulnerability of the French. The Russian campaign had changed the opinion of the monarchies regarding their ability to stand against Napoleon. Like the circling crows which had followed the Grande Armée during the retreat, waiting for an opening to prey on a carcass, the crowned heads of Europe saw in the 1812 defeat a chance to destroy the meaning of the French Revolution, and perhaps acquire additional territories into the bargain. The one thing that they did not forget was that Napoleon had not personally lost a single battle during the campaign. Even so, he could not be in all places at once and there were two or three fronts besides the main one where the French could be hit. What this Mars now lacked was able marshals to cover the fronts where he was not. This his enemies knew and this they would exploit.

Further reading

Arnold, James, *Crisis on the Danube: Napoleon's Austrian Campaign of 1809*, Paragon House, 1990

Bond, Gordon, *The Great Expedition*

Bowden, Scott, *Armies on the Danube 1809*, Emperor's Press, 1989

Chlapowski, Dezydery, *Memoirs of A Polish Lancer*, Emperor's Press, 1992

Clausewitz, Carl von, *The Campaign of 1812 in Russia*, Greenhill Books, 1992

Duffy, Christopher, *Borodino*, Cassell & Co., 1999

Epstein, Robert, *Prince Eugene at War*, Empire Press, 1984

Epstein, Robert M., *Napoleon's Last Victory and the Emergence of Modern War*, University Press of Kansas, 1994

Esposito, Vincent J., and Elting, John R., *Military History & Atlas of the Napoleonic Wars*, Greenhill Books, 1999

Gill, John H., *With Eagles to Glory: Napoleon and his German Allies in the 1809 Campaign*, Greenhill Books, 1992

Josselson, Michael, *The Commander: A Life of Barclay de Tolly*, Oxford University Press, 1980

Nafziger, George, *Napoleon's Invasion of Russia*, Presidio Press, 1988

Palmer, Alan, *Napoleon in Russia: The 1812 Campaign*, Simon & Schuster, 1967

Petre, F. Lorraine, *Napoleon and the Archduke Charles*, Greenhill Books, 1991

Walter, Jakob, (trans. Marc Raiff), *The Diary of a Napoleonic Foot Soldier*, Doubleday, 1991

Index

Other titles in the Essential Histories series

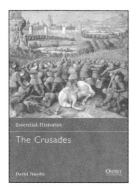

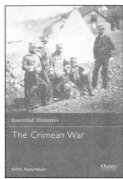

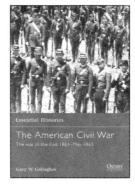

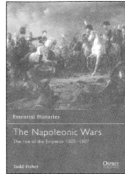

The Crusades
ISBN 1 84176 179 6

available

The Crimean War
ISBN 1 84176 186 9

available

The American Civil War
The war in the East
1861–May 1863
ISBN 1 84176 239 3

available

The Napoleonic Wars
The rise of the Emperor
1805–1807
ISBN 1 84176 205 9

available

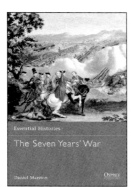

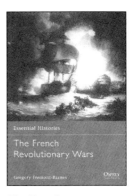

The Seven Years' War
ISBN 1 84176 191 5

available

The American Civil War
The war in the East
1863–1865
ISBN 1 84176 205 9

available

The American Civil War
The war in the West
1861–July 1863
ISBN 1 84176 240 7

available

**The French
Revolutionary Wars**
ISBN 1 84176 283 0

available

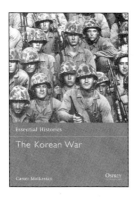

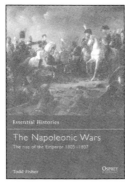

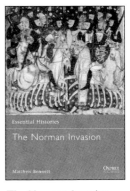

The Korean War
ISBN 1 84176 282 2

available

The Napoleonic Wars
The Empires fight back
1808–1812
ISBN 1 84176 298 9

available

The American Civil War
The war in the West
1863–1865
ISBN 1 84176 242 3

November 2001

The Norman Invasion
ISBN 1 84176 228 8

November 2001

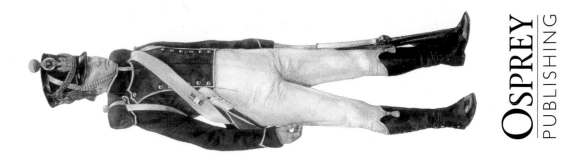

OSPREY PUBLISHING

FIND OUT MORE ABOUT OSPREY

❑ Please send me a FREE trial issue of Osprey Military Journal

❑ Please send me the latest listing of Osprey's publications

❑ I would like to subscribe to Osprey's e-mail newsletter

Title/rank

Name

Address

Postcode/zip

State/country

E-mail

Which book did this card come from?

❑ I am interested in military history

My preferred period of military history is

❑ I am interested in military aviation

My preferred period of military aviation is

I am interested in (please tick all that apply)

❑ general history   ❑ militaria   ❑ model making

❑ wargaming   ❑ re-enactment

Please send to:

USA & Canada:
Osprey Direct USA, c/o Motorbooks International,
PO Box 1, 729 Prospect Avenue, Osceola, WI 54020, USA

UK, Europe and rest of world:
Osprey Direct UK, PO Box 140, Wellingborough,
Northants, NN8 2FA, United Kingdom

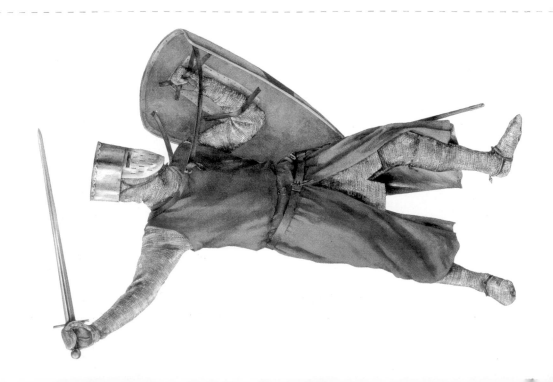

OSPREY
PUBLISHING

www.ospreypublishing.com

call our telephone hotline
for a free information pack

USA & Canada: 1-800-458-0454
UK, Europe and rest of world call:
+44 (0) 1933 443 863

Young Guardsman
Figure taken from *Warrior 22:*
Imperial Guardsman 1799–1815
Published by Osprey
Illustrated by Christa Hook

POSTCARD

Knight, c.1190
Figure taken from *Warrior 1: Norman Knight 950 – 1204AD*
Published by Osprey
Illustrated by Christa Hook